Living a Purposeful Life

Living a Purposeful Life

Searching for Meaning in All the Wrong Places

KALMAN J. KAPLAN

Foreword by Michael Shapiro

WIPF & STOCK • Eugene, Oregon

LIVING A PURPOSEFUL LIFE
Searching for Meaning in All the Wrong Places

Copyright © 2020 Kalman J. Kaplan. All rights reserved. Except for brief quotations in critical publications or reviews, no part of this book may be reproduced in any manner without prior written permission from the publisher. Write: Permissions, Wipf and Stock Publishers, 199 W. 8th Ave., Suite 3, Eugene, OR 97401.

Scripture quotations are taken from the Jewish Publication Society of America Version of the Tanakh, copyright © 1917, 1955 by the Jewish Publication Society. All rights reserved.

Wipf & Stock
An Imprint of Wipf and Stock Publishers
199 W. 8th Ave., Suite 3
Eugene, OR 97401

www.wipfandstock.com

PAPERBACK ISBN: 978-1-7252-6882-1
HARDCOVER ISBN: 978-1-7252-6881-4
EBOOK ISBN: 978-1-7252-6883-8

Manufactured in the U.S.A. 08/21/20

I dedicate this book to my late parents, Lewis C. Kaplan and Edith Saposnik Kaplan, both wonderful human beings and writers in their own right, who taught me that a sense of purpose comes from within, and that meaning cannot be approached directly but is found as a byproduct of living with purpose. And that each life is unique, precious, and of infinite value, on its own terms, regardless of age, wealth, health, social status, or religious-political affiliations or leanings.

I hope I have been successful in transmitting this message to Moriah, and to my descendants, Daniel, Reva, Levi, and Izzy, and theirs.

To everything there is a season, a time to every *purpose* under the heaven.
—Ecclesiastes 3:1

It is legitimate and necessary to wonder whether life has a *meaning*; therefore it is legitimate to meet the problem of suicide face to face.
—Albert Camus, *The Myth of Sisyphus*, Preface

He who has a "why" to live can bear almost any "how."
—Friedrich Nietzsche, *Twilight of the Idols*, Maxims and Arrows, 12

Contents

List of Tables		ix
Foreword by Michael Shapiro		xi
Preface		xiii
Acknowledgments		xv
Introduction		1
1	Two Views of Creation	13
2	Parables against Riddles	18
3	Two Approaches to Life and Death	28
4	Job against Zeno Living Purposively versus Dying in a Search for Meaning	46
5	Purpose versus Meaning in Biblical and Stoic Thought	52
6	Two Clinical Cases	59
7	The Importance of Hope	72
8	Living Purposively versus Searching for Meaning in Ten Areas of Life	81
9	Biblical versus Greek Prophecy Living Purposively against Searching for Meaning	119
Bibliography		133
Index		141

List of Tables

Table 1	Suicides in Greek Tragedy	29
Table 2	Suicides in the Hebrew Bible	36
Table 3	Suicide Preventions in the Hebrew Bible	38
Table 4	Job against Zeno	51
Table 5	Elijah against Ajax	80
Table 6	Jonah against Narcissus	114

Foreword

Kalman Kaplan's distinction between Meaning and Purpose reminds me of an encounter I once had with a Hasidic rabbi on Devon Avenue in Chicago. He had agreed to meet with Confirmation students from my Reform synagogue in Champaign, whom I had brought to Chicago for the weekend to enrich their experience of Jewish life. The *rebbe* was a young man, but to my students his demeanor, sidelocks, and fringes made him seem to them like an ancient sage from remote antiquity. To break the ice, he went around the table asking them, girls included, what they hoped to do in their adult lives. Most of them answered in terms of vocational plans, plans they explained would bring them happiness. He wished them well in fulfilling their aspirations, many of which he deemed quite worthy, but he also issued a caveat about happiness. Happiness, he warned, is not gained by seeking it, but it rather comes unsought when one is fulfilling his or her responsibilities. He did not define these responsibilities, but I understood him to mean, or to include, what Kaplan describes as purposeful or purposive behavior inherent or intrinsic in human existence, that is to say, responsibilities to family and community based on obligations of love and loyalty. For me, Kaplan's understanding of the meaning of life resonated with the rabbi's comment on happiness: both meaning and happiness are byproducts of a life well lived, a life of fulfilled responsibilities. As Kaplan puts it in his final sentence, "*Meaning* cannot be found directly but only as a consequence of living with *purpose*."

Like other scholars critical of Ancient Greece, Kaplan sees the twin poles of glory and shame in Athenian culture as encouraging individuals to actively seek meaning in their lives rather than allow it to emerge from sustained purposeful commitment and conduct. This hunt for significance, he argues, can be dangerous. It can lead one to undertake risky choices in pursuit of honor or public acclaim, and it can lead to the neglect or disparagement of unglamorous domestic and familial commitments, which the poet Linda Pastan in "Who Is It Accuses Us?" calls the truly "dangerous lives." In Kaplan's view, the purposefulness affirmed in the Hebrew Bible is far superior to the search for meaning encouraged in and by ancient Greek culture, a contrast he observes incisively across many areas of life. But Kaplan sees this contrast between the Hellenic and the Hebraic not only as a collision between two ancient civilizations, but as opposing tendencies within our own civilization as well.

MICHAEL SHAPIRO

Preface

I write this preface in April 2020 during the onset of the COVID 19 virus thought to have originated and reach epidemic proportions in Wuhan, the capital city of the Hubei province of China at the end of December, 2019. I think this frightening plague that has fallen on us makes this book especially relevant. As I was rummaging through my library, a book popped out that I had read, or at least skimmed, more than twenty years ago: *Viruses, Plagues, and History*, by Michael Oldstone, professor at that time at the Scripps Research Institute, where he directed the Laboratory of Viral Immunobiology. I vaguely remember skimming it and then putting it aside—I have picked it up again. It was prescient in its warnings.

I remember a number of great works of fiction and history built around the theme of a plague. Samuel Pepys's diaries chronicle the Great Plague of London in 1665–66. Edgar Alan Poe's *The Mask of the Red Death* depicts a plague in an unnamed city in fourteenth-century Europe. In *The Decameron*, Giovanni Bocaccio writes of a small group quarantined in Florence during the Black Death. Thomas Mann writes of a cholera plague in Venice in *Death in Venice* and Albert Camus's *The Plague* tells of an unspecified plague in Oran in French Algiers. Gabriel Garcia Marquez writes of *Love in a Time of Cholera* in an unnamed port city near the Caribbean Sea, probably Cartagena. And of course Sophocles' *Oedipus Rex* begins with a plague overwhelming the city of Thebes, as does the Passover (Pesach) Haggadah, recounting the plagues leading to the exodus of Israel from Egypt. And I am certain that there are many other works of fiction that involve a plague or a catastrophe of one sort or another, for example, the story of Noah and the great flood or of the destruction of Sodom and Gomorrah.

In an age where so many of us have rushed around obsessively in a search for *meaning*, to the point of threatening or even committing suicide or self-destructive acts, we realize suddenly that the choice of life and death is not always ours. As Immanuel Kant said, we are awoken from our "dogmatic slumber." The choice of life and death is not ultimately ours, as much as we may try to take it into our own hands. In whose hands is it then? The Greek *moira* (fate)? Luck? Destiny? Or is our life and death in God's hands, expressed through scientific and medical knowledge. These are weighty questions which suddenly have become immediate. As we will illustrate in chapter 4, Zeno the Stoic overinterprets, indeed catastrophizes, a minor mishap, that is, stubbing or perhaps wrenching his toe, as a sign from the gods that he should depart. The biblical Job has no need for such a destructive search for meaning. He has a *purpose*. To live his life simply. And to do what he can to live his life purposively in the face of great upheaval that has befallen him.

This is what we are all facing now that we are confronted with a calamity. Prior to this, we as a society have been behaving like Zeno, exaggerating slights, catastrophizing people's utterances, and generally behaving like overindulged, shall we say spoiled, brats. We see now that the question of life and death is always what it has been, ultimately not in human control in any simple way. Our choice is how to respond to these assaults. Will we, like Zeno, be incapable of facing adversity, even minor inconveniences; or we will, like Job, fight the plague that has fallen on us with all our strength and all our might?

I pray (yes, *pray*) and hope that by the time this book comes into print, this assault on our lives will have lifted, and that we will have behaved like the biblical Job rather than like Zeno the Stoic. And that we will learn from this.

Acknowledgments

The author would like to acknowledge his indebtedness to Matthew B. Schwartz, Michael Shapiro, and Paul Cantz for their many profound insights and their historical acumen, and to Daniel Algom, David Goldberg, Isabelle Proton, and Michael Zimmerman for giving me the opportunity to bounce ideas off of them.

And of course to my colleagues, Shlomo Shoham of the Buchmann School of Law and Amiram Raviv of the Psychology Department, both of Tel Aviv University, and Anand Kumar and Martin Harrow of the Department of Psychiatry at the University of Illinois College of Medicine, for providing me an academic home over the past fifteen years and for my illuminating conversations with them.

Thank you.

Introduction

THREE OF THE MOST influential books over the last century have focused on *meaning*, the search for it or the lack of it. The 1942 book *The Stranger*, by the French existentialist Albert Camus, stresses the essential *meaninglessness* of life because of the inevitability of death. The protagonist, Meursault, is psychologically detached from the world around him. Seemingly significant events for most people, such as his mother's death or an upcoming marriage, have no meaning for him. Because Meursault seems unable to grieve, he is seen as an outsider, a threat, even a monster. At his subsequent trial for a senseless murder he has committed, the fact that he had no reaction to his mother's death seems to tarnish his image even more than his taking of a life.[1]

In Camus's second book, *The Myth of Sisyphus*, in this same year, he writes about the Greek character Sisyphus, who was assigned the task of pushing a rock up a mountain. Upon reaching the top, the rock would roll down again, leaving Sisyphus to start over. Camus sees Sisyphus as the absurd hero who is condemned to a *meaningless* task, the central concern of *The Myth of Sisyphus*.[2]

Camus claims that there is a fundamental conflict between what we want from the universe (whether it be *meaning*, order, or reason) and what we find in the universe (formless *chaos*). We will never find in life itself the meaning that we want to find. Either we will discover that *meaning* through a leap of faith or we will conclude that life is *meaningless*. Camus asks if coming to the conclusion that life is *meaningless* necessarily leads one to commit suicide. If life has no *meaning*, does that mean life is not worth

1. Camus, *Stranger*.
2. Camus, *Myth of Sisyphus*.

living? If that were the case, are all faced with a choice of making a leap of faith or killing ourselves? Camus suggests a third possibility: that we can accept and live in a world devoid of *meaning*, hardly an attractive option. It should be pointed out that Camus wrote both of these books from Nazi-occupied France during World War II. This was a very pessimistic period in France as Germany had invaded in May of 1940.

Man's Search for Meaning was published somewhat later, in 1959, by Viktor Frankl, who writes that he developed his logotherapy out of his experiences in Nazi concentration camps in Nazi-occupied Poland. Frankl argues that man's search for *meaning* is the primary motivation in his life and not a secondary rationalization of instinctual drives. Frankl on the surface seems less philosophically pessimistic than Camus. But as the title of his book clearly states, *meaning* is something that must be searched for. It is not intrinsic in one's personality.[3]

However, is this really true? Or does it represent an attempt by a therapist to impose a *meaning* structure on an individual? This is a criticism levied at logotherapy in 1960 by no less than Rollo May, one of the founders of existential psychology.[4] In May's view, Frankl applied (perhaps even imposed) a specific *meaning* structure on a patient when he/she did not have a particular goal. May thus feels despite its advantages, Frankl's logotherapy "hovers close to authoritarianism."

Suicide is rampant in today's world, and many people report feeling that their lives are without *purpose*. Yet a *search for meaning* can actually be quite destructive. Consider the murders committed by Charles Manson's *Helter Skelter* gang as the tumultuous 1960s were coming to an end. Manson often spoke to the members of his "family" about "Helter Skelter" in the months leading up to the murders of Sharon Tate and Leno and Rosemary LaBianca in August 1969. "Helter Skelter" referred to an apocalyptic war arising from racial tensions between blacks and whites and referred specifically to songs in an album by the Beatles entitled *The White Album*, and to the book of Revelation in the Christian New Testament. Manson and his followers were convicted of the murders on the basis of the theory by the prosecution that they were part of a plan to trigger the Helter Skelter scenario.[5] Yet, were they not searching for *meaning*?

In direct contrast to these books is a more recent very popular work, *The Purpose Driven Life* by Rick Warren, published in 2002. Warren is pastor

---

3. Frankl, *Man's Search for Meaning*.
4. May, *Existential Psychology*, 41–42.
5. The reader is referred to an excellent book by Vincent Bugliosi, lead prosecutor in the Tate–LaBianca murder trial, to explain the series of murders committed by the Manson Family. Bugliosi described his theory at trial and in his 1974 book, *Helter Skelter: The True Story of the Manson Murders*.

of a megachurch in sunny Southern California, a very different place than the gray Nazi-occupied Europe, and indeed the death camps themselves in Frankl's case. What is important for Warren is not *searching for meaning* but *living one's life purposively*.[6] A similar stance is taken by Kay Warren in her very positive 2012 book, *Choose Joy, Because Happiness Is Not Enough*.[7] While both books are written in a specific christological framework, their thoughts express a more general biblical view of life. Could the fact that the Warrens are writing in sunny California rather than a grey, cloudy European context explain the difference in their views. Yet, this difference in locale alone cannot explain this difference; after all, the previously discussed horrific murders committed by the Manson gang occurred in sunny Southern California. It is thus possible to be destructively obsessed with a search for *meaning*—even in "sunny Southern California."

So what is the difference? What is the difference between *searching for meaning* and *living purposely*, and where does this difference come from? Perhaps it lies in the observations of the French writer Alexis de Tocqueville in his classic work *Democracy in America*. He puts it this way with regard to how his experience in America altered his view of religion.

> In France I had always seen the spirit of religion and the spirit of freedom pursuing courses diametrically opposed to each other; but in America I found that they were intimately united, and they reigned in common over the same country.[8]

While Camus' and Frankl's thought do not seem to be emerging from a biblical worldview, the Warrens' view does, and it is grounded firmly in biblical thought. Three separate biblical verses record the Israelites' acceptance of the obligations that the Hebrew Scriptures (Torah) impose on them.

When Moses first ascends Mount Sinai, God commands him to tell the people that if they accept the covenant, God will make them a "kingdom of priests and a holy nation."[9] Upon hearing these words, the people respond, "All that God has said, we will do."[10]

Later in the text, after Moses relates specific divine rules to the people, they again say, "All of the things that God has said, we will do."[11] A few verses later, after Moses writes and reads aloud the words of Scriptures, the people

---

6. Warren, *Purpose Driven Life*.
7. Warren, *Choose Joy*.
8. De Tocqueville, *Democracy in America*, 394.
9. Exod 19:6.
10. Exod 19:8.
11. Exod 24:3.

utter the phrase *na'aseh v'nishma*.[12] Although this literally is translated as "we will do and we will hear," it has often been interpreted as "we will *first* do and *then* we will understand." In other words, *meaning* does not need to be searched for, it is a consequence of living a *purposeful* life.

Nicholas Wolterstorff, former Noah Porter Professor Emeritus of Philosophical Theology at Yale University, argues this same point.

> The ancient Greek writers had a tragic view of life. Theirs was a culture of honor and shame; they admired the hero. But the hero often found himself enmeshed in a situation where death provided the only alternative to living in shame. The fates had decreed. There was no other way out. . .[However] the biblical God is not one who decrees our fate but one who has created each of us as a creature of worth, and who loves us. . .. In this world, heroism is not called for; it's enough that we be grateful and make good use of the life that's given us.[13]

The great Russian-Jewish philosopher Lev Shestov puts the problem this way in his work *Athens and Jerusalem.*

> The Creator of the world has Himself become subordinate to Necessity which He created and which, without at all seeking or desiring it has become the sovereign of the universe. . . We must try to stand up against Necessity itself, try to free the living and feeling Parmenides from dead and altogether indifferent power.[14]

While *searching for meaning* can lead us terribly astray and indeed create terrible havoc, *living purposively* represents the essence of a biblical approach to life. My own work argues this very point and offers a biblically based psychotherapy as an antidote to the suicide crisis in contemporary society.[15] Perhaps the very term "suicide prevention" is often too negative, too little, and too late. What seems much more effective is a culture of "life promotion," where people grow up validating life and not death, living life *purposively* rather than in an endless search for *meaning* that too often can lead to destructive behaviors, even suicide.

Before we pursue this question in more detail, let us discuss a curious phenomenon that has emerged in America (and indeed much of the Western world over the last twenty-five years): a dramatic increase in the popularity of running marathons. This has occurred despite the publication

---

12. Exod 24:3.
13. Kaplan and Schwartz, *Psychology of Hope*, xiii.
14. Shestov, *Athens and Jerusalem*, 85–86, 91–92.
15. Kaplan and Cantz, *Biblical Psychotherapy.*

of medical articles reporting on injuries to runners of all experience, with yearly incidence rates for injury reported by Fredericson and Misra[16] in 2007 to be as high as 90 percent in those training for marathons.

For example, one study in 1998 by Marti and his associates[17] reports survey results indicating that of 4,358 male joggers studied during the course of a year, 45.8 percent had sustained at least one injury. They strongly suggest a healthy regimen lies in the range of 10–25 kilometers per week. Macera and her associates[18] issue similar warnings in 1991, indicating that male marathon runners were almost twice as likely to report lower extremity musculoskeletal problems in the month after the race, and female marathon runners were four times more likely to report such problems.

More recent research articles also point to potential dangers in the running of marathons. In 2014 Saragiotto et. al. report a review of 4,671 pooled participants which pointed to previous injury within the last twelve months prior to their running as the major risk factor for subsequent injury.[19] Nathan reports the results of a questionnaire study indicating a significant association ($p < .003$) between running time and injury while running the 2012 London Marathon. Runners who completed the marathon in less than four hours were less likely to sustain an injury than those finishing in greater than four hours.[20] Perhaps those runners finishing in less time were better trained or more physically fit to begin with.

Tellingly, Nathan in 2013 points out the dramatic increase in the popularity and participation in marathons noted by Fredericson and Misra and suggests, "it would be interesting to consider what the reason for this increase may be." And we echo this question: "Where does the idea of the marathon race come from?"

THE RUN OF PHEIDIPPIDES

The marathon derives from the story of Pheidippides (530–490 BCE), an Athenian herald or "courier"[21] who was sent to Sparta to request help when the Persians landed at Marathon, Greece. Whether this actually took place is debated by scholars. But in any case, here is the basic story. Athenian runner

16. Fredericson and Misra, "Epidemiology and Aetiology of Marathon Running Injuries."
17. Marti et al., "On the Epidemiology of Running Injuries."
18. Macera et al., "Postrace Morbidity among Runners."
19. Saragiotto et al., "What Are the Main Risk Factors?"
20. Nathan, "Injury Prevention in Marathon Runners."
21. Herodotus, *Histories*, vol. 3; Larcher, *Notes on Herodotus*.

Pheidippides ran about 240 kilometers (150 miles) in two days to ask the Spartans for help against Persian invaders. He seems to have failed in his request, but his run is completely understandable, and laudable. But then we come to more perplexing part of the story. Pheidippides then runs 40 kilometers (25 miles) from the battlefield near Marathon to Athens to announce the Greek victory over Persia in the Battle of Marathon (490 BCE) with the exclamation "We win!" in Greek. He then collapses and dies. On the surface, this story seems to be very heroic. In fact, the English poet Robert Browning gives us a highly romanticized version of the story in his 1879 poem *Pheidippides*, equating his death (joy bursting his heart) with bliss.

> So, when Persia was dust, all cried, "To Acropolis!
> Run, Pheidippides, one race more! the meed is thy due!
> Athens is saved, thank Pan, go shout!" He flung down his shield
> Ran like fire once more: and the space 'twixt the fennel-field
> And Athens was stubble again, a field which a fire runs through,
> Till in he broke: "Rejoice, we conquer!" Like wine through clay,
> Joy in his blood bursting his heart,—the bliss.[22]

And this brings us to a perplexing part of the story. Why did the Greek Pheidippides push himself beyond his endurance to be the first to announce the Greek victory over the Persians? The Greeks had defeated the Persians at Marathon. Why was he driven to be the first to announce this news? On the surface, it did not have any obvious instrumental value. The Greeks had won. What gain did the Greeks in Athens derive from receiving this knowledge immediately, as opposed to the next day? Their forces had been victorious at Marathon—they had defeated the Persians. And even if the Greeks had received some benefit from immediate knowledge of their victory at Marathon,[23] why did not Pheidippides ride on a horse? And even if there was a compelling reason for this, why is Pheidippides' clearly physically dangerous act valorized to this day, with people all over the world training in an attempt to emulate this act, despite, as mentioned above, the documented medical risks attendant to it?

We cannot avoid the interpretation that this ancient story fed into the ancient Greek sense of the heroic. In his superb book *The Glory of Hera: Greek Mythology and the Greek Family*, Phillip Slater tells us much of interest about the ancient Greeks and perhaps modern Western life. The Greeks were as creative a people as have ever lived and seemed to search for

---

22. Browning, *Pheidippides*.

23. A version of the story suggests that this knowledge may have allowed the Athenian army to march to the beaches on the west side of the city and prevent a second Persian attack.

meaning in everything they did. They were not content with living simple lives but oftentimes took on gargantuan tasks which resulted in a great deal of upheaval and unpleasantness and oftentimes to disaster. Slater puts it this way: "The Greeks were quarrelsome as friends, treacherous as neighbors, brutal as masters, faithless as servants, shallow as lovers—all of which was in part redeemed by their intelligence and creativity."[24]

And much of contemporary Western society seems to be acting exactly like these ancient Greeks, looking for exaggerated activities, often quite dangerous and self-destructive, to find *meaning* in otherwise empty lives. They are willing to do this even to the point of risking their own health and even at times their lives. And running marathons is a prime example of this phenomenon even though it can be detrimental to one's health, as the medical evidence previously cited by Fredericson and Misra clearly suggests. But running the marathon is not unique in this regard. A good number of people engage in quite dangerous activities in an attempt to gain a sense of accomplishment, indeed *meaning*, missing in their everyday lives, which seem to be empty of *purpose*. Mindlessly emulating Pheidippides' run seems a prime example of this. And even if Pheidippides' action did have a specific *purpose*, rather than reflect an amorphous need for *meaning*, why did he not ride a horse as did Paul Revere. We will examine Paul Revere's story now.

THE RIDE OF PAUL REVERE

Paul Revere was a silversmith, engraver, early industrialist, and patriot in the American Revolution against Britain. He was obviously not an ancient Greek, but a biblical man, by all accounts a fairly typical early New England Christian. Paul Revere seemed to have been a regular attendee in Boston's New Brick Church and was most likely quite familiar with stories in the Hebrew Bible and in the Christian New Testament.

Paul Revere is best known for his midnight ride to alert the colonial militia in April 1775 to the approach of British forces before the battles of Lexington and Concord, as dramatized in Henry Wadsworth Longfellow's poem, *Paul Revere's Ride*. He did not seem to be searching for *meaning*. Rather, his action had a *purpose*. Most importantly, Paul Revere did not die, nor did he push himself beyond his endurance.

> Listen, my children, and you shall hear
> Of the midnight ride of Paul Revere,
> On the eighteenth of April, in Seventy-Five:

---

24. Slater, *Glory of Hera*, 4.

Hardly a man is now alive
Who remembers that famous day and year.

He said to his friend, "If the British march
By land or sea from the town to-night,
Hang a lantern aloft in the belfry-arch
Of the North-Church-tower, as a signal-light,—
One if by land, and two if by sea.
And I on the opposite shore will be,
Ready to ride and spread the alarm
Through every Middlesex village and farm,
For the country-folk to be up and to arm."
Then he said, "Good night!" and with muffled oar
Silently rowed to the Charlestown shore,
Just as the moon rose over the bay,
Where swinging wide at her moorings lay
The Somerset, British man-of-war:
A phantom ship, with each mast and spar
Across the moon, like a prison-bar,
And a huge black hulk, that was magnified
By its own reflection in the tide.

Meanwhile, his friend, through alley and street
Wanders and watches with eager ears,
Till in the silence around him he hears
The muster of men at the barrack door,
The sound of arms, and the tramp of feet,
And the measured tread of the grenadiers
Marching down to their boats on the shore.

Then he climbed to the tower of the church,
Up the wooden stairs, with stealthy tread,
To the belfry-chamber overhead,
And startled the pigeons from their perch
On the sombre rafters, that round him made
Masses and moving shapes of shade,—
By the trembling ladder, steep and tall,
To the highest window in the wall,
Where he paused to listen and look down
A moment on the roofs of the town,
And the moonlight flowing over all.

Beneath, in the churchyard, lay the dead,
In their night-encampment on the hill,

Wrapped in silence so deep and still
That he could hear, like a sentinel's tread,
The watchful night-wind, as it went
Creeping along from tent to tent,
And seeming to whisper, "All is well!"
A moment only he feels the spell
Of the place and the hour, and the secret dread
Of the lonely belfry and the dead.
For suddenly all his thoughts are bent
On a shadowy something far away,
Where the river widens to meet the bay,—
A line of black, that bends and floats
On the rising tide, like a bridge of boats.

Meanwhile, impatient to mount and ride,
Booted and spurred, with a heavy stride,
On the opposite shore walked Paul Revere.
Now he patted his horse's side,
Now gazed on the landscape far and near,
Then impetuous stamped the earth,
And turned and tightened his saddle-girth;
But mostly he watched with eager search
The belfry-tower of the old North Church,
As it rose above the graves on the hill,
Lonely and spectral and sombre and still.
And lo! as he looks, on the belfry's height,
A glimmer, and then a gleam of light!
He springs to the saddle, the bridle he turns,
But lingers and gazes, till full on his sight
A second lamp in the belfry burns!

A hurry of hoofs in a village-street,
A shape in the moonlight, a bulk in the dark,
And beneath from the pebbles, in passing, a spark
Struck out by a steed that flies fearless and fleet:
That was all! And yet, through the gloom and the light,
The fate of a nation was riding that night;
And the spark struck out by that steed, in his flight,
Kindled the land into flame with its heat.

He has left the village and mounted the steep,
And beneath him, tranquil and broad and deep,
Is the Mystic, meeting the ocean tides;
And under the alders, that skirt its edge,

Now soft on the sand, now loud on the ledge,
Is heard the tramp of his steed as he rides.

It was twelve by the village clock
When he crossed the bridge into Medford town.
He heard the crowing of the cock,
And the barking of the farmer's dog,
And felt the damp of the river-fog,
That rises when the sun goes down.

It was one by the village clock,
When he galloped into Lexington.
He saw the gilded weathercock
Swim in the moonlight as he passed,
And the meeting-house windows, blank and bare,
Gaze at him with a spectral glare,
As if they already stood aghast
At the bloody work they would look upon.

It was two by the village clock,
When he came to the bridge in Concord town.
He heard the bleating of the flock,
And the twitter of birds among the trees,
And felt the breath of the morning breeze
Blowing over the meadows brown.
And one was safe and asleep in his bed
Who at the bridge would be first to fall,
Who that day would be lying dead,
Pierced by a British musket-ball.

You know the rest. In the books you have read,
How the British Regulars fired and fled,—
How the farmers gave them ball for ball,
From behind each fence and farmyard-wall,
Chasing the red-coats down the lane,
Then crossing the fields to emerge again
Under the trees at the turn of the road,
And only pausing to fire and load.

So through the night rode Paul Revere;
And so through the night went his cry of alarm
To every Middlesex village and farm,—
A cry of defiance, and not of fear,
A voice in the darkness, a knock at the door,

And a word that shall echo forevermore!
For, borne on the night-wind of the Past,
Through all our history, to the last,
In the hour of darkness and peril and need,
The people will waken and listen to hear
The hurrying hoof-beats of that steed,
And the midnight message of Paul Revere.

Paul Revere's career and reputation were somewhat tarnished in the latter part of the war,[25] but he went back to his family business, and broadened his metalworking to include a bell foundry in 1792. He helped provide a replacement bell for his congregation to which he belonged, the New Brick Church in Boston. Between 1792 and his death in 1818, Revere's company—Revere and Son—made more than one hundred bells.

The difference in these two legends is very much the point of this book. We must ask again, why did the Greek Pheidippides push himself beyond his endurance to be the first to announce the Greek victory over the Persians? Why did he need to be the first to announce this news? Did this act which led to his death really have any obvious instrumental value? The Greeks had won. What secondary gain did Pheidippides derive from this action that led him to so overtax himself that he collapsed and died? Why did he run rather than ride a horse? Finally, were Pheidippides' actions indicative of an ancient Greek way of looking at the world and indeed of constructing meaning? Seemingly, for the ancient Greeks, nothing could be nobler than dying after performing a heroic deed for one's country. But was this really what was going on? Why did Browning romanticize Pheidippides' fatal run?

Contrast this to the story of Paul Revere, who had a much more pressing message to transmit. He needed to warn the revolutionary militia that "the British were coming." Yet Paul Revere did not seem to be looking to be a hero. He was living within himself, simply doing his job, and afterwards seemed quite content to go back to his own life. This is where the biblical Paul Revere seemed to find his *purpose*. He lived within himself and did not need to search for *meaning* in exaggerated activities. In contrast, the ancient Greek Pheidippides extended himself beyond his endurance, collapsed and died. Was this difference incidental, or was it indicative of the difference in the different ways classical Greeks and biblical Jews understood *purpose* and

---

25. Specifically, Paul Revere was charged with insubordination for his actions during the Penobscot Expedition, a chaotic naval operation that cost the Continental forces hundreds of lives in 1779. Revere was ultimately cleared of any wrongdoing, but any career in the military was permanently blocked.

meaning?—two terms which are often used interchangeably, but which we will are argue are quite distinct live motives.

This is not to say that we all don't want to lead fulfilling lives and to leave some mark or legacy after we pass from this earth, indeed have some sort of *purpose*. But people without an inner sense of *purpose* seem to often choose very dangerous and even destructive activities in their attempt to find *meaning*. This search for the heroic may well shorten their lives or leave them injured badly, either physically or spiritually, or both.

1

Two Views of Creation

No people seemed to search more for *meaning* in their lives than did the ancient and classical Greeks. In his superb book *The Glory of Hera: Greek Mythology and the Greek Family*, Phillip Slater tells us much of interest about the ancient Greeks. They were as creative a people as have ever lived and seemed to search for *meaning* in everything they did. They were not content with living simple lives but oftentimes took on gargantuan tasks which resulted in a great deal of upheaval and unpleasantness, and oftentimes to disaster. Slater puts it this way: "The Greeks were quarrelsome as friends, treacherous as neighbors, brutal as masters, faithless as servants, shallow as lovers—all of which was in part redeemed by their intelligence and creativity."[1] Daily life had no *purpose* for the ancient Greeks; they were searching for *meaning* in exceptionally difficult tasks.

The biblical human being, in contrast, is not driven to search for *meaning in* this way. One's *purpose* is inherent in daily life. He does not have to search for it. The God of the Hebrew Bible makes the human being, man and woman, in his own image.

---

1. Slater, *Glory of Hera*, 4

> And God said: "Let us make man in His own image; in the image of God, created He him,; male and female created he them.[2]

He then breathes life into man.

> Then the Lord God formed man of the dust of the ground and breathed into his nostrils the breath of life; and man became a living soul.[3]

Life has an inherent *purpose*. Man must be a steward of God's creation.[4]

> And God said, Let us make man in our image, after our likeness: and let them have dominion over the fish of the sea, and over the fowl of the air, and over the cattle, and over all the earth, and over every creeping thing that creepeth upon the earth.[5]

A passage in Exodus restates the *purposeful* nature of life. God has a *purpose* for everyone.

> But I have raised you up for this very purpose, that I might show you my power and that my name might be proclaimed in all the earth."[6]

The *purposeful* nature of life is stated again in the first book of Samuel. We find *purpose* by serving God.

> We fulfill our *purpose* of glorifying God also by living our lives in relationship and faithful service to Him.[7]

To gains some perspective on this difference, let us compare the creation narrative in Hesiod's *Theogony* with that of the Hebrew Scriptures. These two creation stories embody two radically different worldviews. Nature precedes the gods in the Greek version, but God precedes nature in the biblical account. As Bruno Snell argues, the differences in the respective orderings are not just chronological, but logical and psychological as well.[8]

---

2. Gen 1:27
3. Gen 2:7.
4. Gen 2:7.
5. Gen 1:26–27.
6. Exod 9:16.
7. 1 Sam 12:24.
8. Snell, *Discovery of the Mind*.

THE GREEK CREATION NARRATIVE

According to Hesiod, in the beginning there was *chaos*, which has often been interpreted as a moving formless mass, from which the cosmos and the gods originated.[9] The noun *xaos* refers to infinite space or time or the nether abyss, while the verb *xao* denotes "to destroy utterly.[10] There is the implication that *chaos* must be subdued and controlled for the world to be formed. *Purpose* is not inherent in creation. It must be searched for. *The human being must search for meaning!*

In this Olympian *Theogony*, nature exists before the gods. First Sky rules over the entire world.[11] Sky (the male Ouranos) marries Earth (the female Gaia) and produces, first the hundred-handed monsters, and then the Cyclopes.[12] The family pathology then immediately commences, as the father takes the children away from the mother. "Sky tied them (the Cyclopes) up and threw them into Tartarus, a dark and gloomy place in Hades as far from earth as earth is from the sky and again had children by Earth, the so-called Titans."[13] Such action breeds reaction.

> Grieved at the loss of the children who were thrown into Tartarus, Earth persuaded the Titans to attack their father and gave Cronus a steel sickle ... Cronus cut off his father's genitals and threw them into the sea ... Having thus eliminated their Father the Titans brought back their brother who had been hurled to Tartarus and gave the rule to Cronus.[14]

Father is set against son, and son must rebel against father in his search for *meaning*. When Earth and Sky foretold that Cronus would lose the rule to his own son, he devoured his offspring as they were born.[15] The infant Zeus is saved through a ruse. When Zeus reaches adulthood, he makes war on Cronus and the Titans, and defeats him, fulfilling the prophecy of Earth and Sky.[16] The drama of infanticide continues. Zeus himself is informed that his own son would displace him. To forestall this, he devours the mother Metis with the embryo in her womb.[17]

9. Hesiod, *Theogony* l.116.
10. Liddell et al., *Greek-English Lexicon*.
11. Apollodorus, *Library* 1.1.1.
12. Apollodorus, *Library* 1.1.2.
13. Apollodorus, *Library* 1.1.3.
14. Apollodorus, *Library* 1.1.4.
15. Apollodorus, *Library* 1.1.5.
16. Apollodorus, *Library* 1.2.1.
17. Apollodorus, *Library* 1.3.6.

However, the playwright Aeschylus adds that Zeus is not all-powerful, subject himself to the natural force of Necessity, which itself is controlled by the Fates and the Furies.[18]

In summary then:

1. Earth and Sky exist prior to the gods and in fact create them. The world begins in *chaos*, which must be subdued.
2. The Earth-mother is a very ambivalent source. She gives life but also destroys it. Such a view creates an ambivalent human attitude towards her, vacillating between paralyzing idealization of and submission to the earth and rebellious destructiveness with regard to it. We will discuss this in far greater detail in chapter 8.
3. Life is consumed with a search for *meaning*, not in daily life, but in grandiose tasks and adventures.

THE BIBLICAL CREATION NARRATIVE

The biblical account of creation is very different. God precedes and indeed creates nature. Nature representing the rules which God has put into place to create some order in the physical world he has created. "In the beginning God created the heaven and the earth." God then proceeds to create form out of the unformed (*tohu vovohu*)—again, not by subduing *chaos* as in the Greek account. To emphasize, the biblical *unformed* is not equivalent to the Greek *chaos*. Therefore, nature does not have to be subdued, but shaped. God is not seen a tyrant but as a potter.

First, lightness is divided from darkness. God then divides water from the land. At this point, God begins to prepare this world for the entrance of man. First, God has the earth bring forth vegetation. He then places living creatures in the sea and fowls in the sky. Now God places living creatures on the earth, cattle, creeping things, and other beasts.[19] The world is now ready for man in God's plan. God creates the human being, male and female, his ultimate handiwork, in God's own image and gives them dominion over all in nature God has created.[20]

The Bible describes the world and all that is in it as created by God in love. Humankind are given dominion over all, and the first people are placed in the garden of Eden "to dress and keep it." It is incumbent on humanity not to wantonly destroy. Having dominion does not entitle man to

---

18. Aeschylus, *Prometheus Bound*, ll. 514–17.
19. Gen 1.
20. Gen 1:26.

misuse nature. Nature is not presented as something alien to man; it is to be neither worshiped nor raped, but instead tended and cared for lovingly and carefully.

The following points stand out in these biblical narratives:

1. God exists prior to the heaven and earth and in fact creates them. The world is unformed (*tohu vovohu*) and must be given form and structure rather than subdued.
2. Earth is not seen in sexually differentiated terms. There is no sense of an Earth-mother. The earth is not to be ravaged but it also is not to be worshiped. The biblical God creates man and woman to tend and care for the world he has created. People can and do make changes to the world to improve it but must not do this in a callous or needlessly destructive way. This too will be discussed in greater detail in chapter 8.
3. Life is not about a fruitless search for *meaning*. It is inherently *purposeful*. One does not have to pursue grandiose goals. Living one's own life in a modest and *purposeful* way is sufficient.

2

Parables against Riddles

IN MANY WAYS, THE ancient Greeks saw life as a *riddle* to be solved. In contrast, biblical man saw life as a *parable* to be lived. The first view pushes towards an endless search for *meaning*; the second towards a *purposeful* life.

THE ANCIENT GREEKS LOVE RIDDLES

Riddles are largely unintelligible and demand a search for *meaning*. They are admired in ancient Greek thought specifically because they are less intelligible than the simple presentation of facts and transmit *no meaning*. In his probing discussion of the non-informative aspect of Apollo's speech, the classicist Bruce Heiden (2005) raises the question of whether Apollo's noncommunicative oracles served another function. He cites Sophocles' fragment 771 in this regard.

> And I thoroughly understand that the god is this way:
> To the wise, always a poser of riddles in divine speech,
> but to the foolish a teacher of lessons, trivial and concise.

Heiden goes on to argue that "the different addressees for whom Apollo's speeches are either lessons or riddles do not exercise different linguistic competencies, but different degrees of wisdom, and the acquisition of the positive *meaning* of the teaching surprisingly accords with stupidity, while the riddle, whose characteristic is denial of *meaning*, accords with positive wisdom."[1]

THE HEBREW BIBLE LOVES PARABLES

Consider in contrast Scripture's description of Abraham at the end of his life as being "satisfied with days." Parables, while metaphorical, give clear life lessons, perhaps better accepted than naked truth. They can be seen as providing a guide for *purposeful* living.

> Truth, naked and cold, had been turned away from every door in the village. Her nakedness frightened the people. When Parable found her, she was huddled in a corner, shivering and hungry. Taking pity on her, Parable gathered her up and took her home. There, she dressed Truth in story, warmed her and sent her out again. Clothed in story, Truth knocked again at the doors and was readily welcomed into the villagers' houses. They invited her to eat at their tables and warm herself by their fires. Ever since that time, Truth and Parable have gone hand in hand and they are made welcome wherever they go. "And do you see," concluded the Preacher of Dubno, "I do not change the truth, nor try to hide it within my stories. I merely dress it up in beautiful clothing so that people will welcome it into their hearts"[2]

In this context, let us compare two very well-known fables: the story of Rumpelstiltskin versus that of the emperor with no clothes.

RUMPELSTILTSKIN

Consider the famous riddle of Rumpelstiltskin, which is not Greek at all but illustrates a fruitless search for *meaning*. We follow the Brothers Grimm version.[3]

> A poor miller had a beautiful daughter. Once he had occasion to speak to the king and, to give himself an air of importance, boasted that his daughter could spin straw into gold. The king ordered the miller to bring the girl to the palace. If she succeeded, he would make her his queen; if not, she would be put to

---

1. Heiden, *Eavesdropping on Apollo*, 236–37.
2. Baltuck, *Apples from Heaven*, 71.
3. From Pullman, *Fairy Tales from the Brothers Grimm*, 221–25.

death. The next day the girl came and was placed in a room full of straw and ordered to spin the straw into gold. The poor girl, of course, had no idea what to do. Suddenly the door opened, and a little man stepped into the room. Learning of the girl's dilemma, the little man asked, "What will you give me if I spin this straw into gold?" The girl volunteered her necklace, and the little man spun all the straw into gold. The king was thrilled but also greedy. On the next day, he again placed the girl in a room full of straw with same demand. Once again the little man appeared and offered to spin the straw into gold in exchange, this time for the girl's ring. The greedy king repeated his demand on the third day. Again, the little man came, but this time the girl had no more baubles to give him. "Well then," said the little man, "will you promise to give me your first-born child if you become queen?" Desperately frightened, the girl agreed. When the king returned the next day, the room was once more filled with gold, and he married the miller's daughter.

A year later, a beautiful child was born. The queen had quite forgotten the little man, but he came and demanded the child as promised. Terrified, the queen offered him all sorts of wealth but could not dissuade him from demanding the child. She wept so bitterly that the little man finally felt sorry for her. He agreed to give her three days. If she could discover his name, she could keep the child.

For two days, the queen guessed a long list of names but could not discover the true name. On the third day, one of her agents came in and reported that he had passed a little house far away in a forest on a mountain, where he saw a little man dancing around a fire and singing a song that ended with the words, "And little knows the royal dame that Rumpelstiltskin is my name."

When the little man returned on the third day and heard the queen's correct answer, he grew so enraged that he stamped his foot into the ground up to his waist, and then seizing his left leg tore himself apart.

The central riddle in the story is the little man's name, but the story contains other characteristic features as well—the magical entry of the little man and his inhuman appearance, the remarkable greed and cruelty of the king, the importance of gold, and the lack of decency. There is little to learn from the story except that the world is a frightening and irrationally insecure place. The very search for the *meaning* of the riddle is destructive. A riddle such as this leaves the listener feeling powerless; there is nothing one can do to escape a terrible situation.

THE EMPEROR'S NEW CLOTHES

Consider in contrast the famous parable of "The Emperor's New Clothes" by Hans Christian Anderson.[4]

> Many years ago there was an Emperor so exceedingly fond of new clothes that he spent all his money on being well dressed. He cared nothing about reviewing his soldiers, going to the theatre, or going for a ride in his carriage, except to show off his new clothes. He had a coat for every hour of the day, and instead of saying, as one might, about any other ruler, "The King's in council," here they always said, "The Emperor's in his dressing room."
>
> In the great city where he lived, life was always joyous. Every day many strangers came to town, and among them one day came two swindlers. They let it be known they were weavers, and they said they could weave the most magnificent fabrics imaginable. Not only were their colors and patterns uncommonly fine, but clothes made of this cloth had a wonderful way of becoming invisible to anyone who was unfit for his office, or who was unusually stupid.
>
> "Those would be just the clothes for me," thought the Emperor. "If I wore them I would be able to discover which men in my empire are unfit for their posts. And I could tell the wise men from the fools. Yes, I certainly must get some of the stuff woven for me right away." He paid the two swindlers a large sum of money to start work at once.
>
> They set up two looms and pretended to weave, though there was nothing on the looms. All the finest silk and the purest old thread which they demanded went into their traveling bags, while they worked the empty looms far into the night. "I'd like to know how those weavers are getting on with the cloth," the Emperor thought, but he felt slightly uncomfortable when he remembered that those who were unfit for their position would not be able to see the fabric. It couldn't have been that he doubted himself, yet he thought he'd rather send someone else to see how things were going. The whole town knew about the cloth's peculiar power, and all were impatient to find out how stupid their neighbors were.

4. Andersen, *Emperor's New Clothes*.

"I'll send my honest old minister to the weavers," the Emperor decided. "He'll be the best one to tell me how the material looks, for he's a sensible man and no one does his duty better." So the honest old minister went to the room where the two swindlers sat working away at their empty looms. "Heaven help me," he thought as his eyes flew wide open, "I can't see anything at all." But he did not say so.

Both the swindlers begged him to be so kind as to come near to approve the excellent pattern, the beautiful colors. They pointed to the empty looms, and the poor old minister stared as hard as he dared. He couldn't see anything, because there was nothing to see. "Heaven have mercy," he thought. "Can it be that I'm a fool? I'd have never guessed it, and not a soul must know. Am I unfit to be the minister? It would never do to let on that I can't see the cloth."

"Don't hesitate to tell us what you think of it," said one of the weavers. "Oh, it's beautiful—it's enchanting." The old minister peered through his spectacles. "Such a pattern, what colors!" I'll be sure to tell the Emperor how delighted I am with it."

"We're pleased to hear that," the swindlers said. They proceeded to name all the colors and to explain the intricate pattern. The old minister paid the closest attention, so that he could tell it all to the Emperor. And so he did.

The swindlers at once asked for more money, more silk and gold thread, to get on with the weaving. But it all went into their pockets. Not a thread went into the looms, though they worked at their weaving as hard as ever.

The Emperor presently sent another trustworthy official to see how the work progressed and how soon it would be ready. The same thing happened to him that had happened to the minister. He looked and he looked, but as there was nothing to see in the loom; he couldn't see anything. "Isn't it a beautiful piece of goods?" the swindlers asked him, as they displayed and described their imaginary pattern.

"I know I'm not stupid," the man thought, "so it must be that I'm unworthy of my good office. That's strange. I mustn't let anyone find it out, though." So he praised the material he did not see. He declared he was delighted with the beautiful colors and the exquisite pattern. To the Emperor he said, "It held me spellbound."

All the town was talking of this splendid cloth, and the Emperor wanted to see it for himself while it was still in the looms. Attended by a band of chosen men, among whom were his two old trusted officials-the ones who had been to the weavers-he set out to see the two swindlers. He found them weaving with might and main, but without a thread in their looms.

"Magnificent," said the two officials already duped. "Just look, Your Majesty, what colors! What a design!" They pointed to the empty looms, each supposing that the others could see the stuff.

"What's this?" thought the Emperor. "I can't see anything. This is terrible!

Am I a fool? Am I unfit to be the Emperor? What a thing to happen to me of all people!—Oh! It's very pretty," he said. "It has my highest approval." And he nodded approbation at the empty loom. Nothing could make him say that he couldn't see anything.

His whole retinue stared and stared. One saw no more than another, but they all joined the Emperor in exclaiming, "Oh! It's very pretty," and they advised him to wear clothes made of this wonderful cloth especially for the great procession he was soon to lead. "Magnificent! Excellent! Unsurpassed!" were bandied from mouth to mouth, and everyone did his best to seem well pleased. The Emperor gave each of the swindlers a cross to wear in his buttonhole, and the title of Sir Weaver. Before the procession the swindlers sat up all night and burned more than six candles, to show how busy they were finishing the Emperor's new clothes. They pretended to take the cloth off the loom. They made cuts in the air with huge scissors. And at last they said, "Now the Emperor's new clothes are ready for him."

Then the Emperor himself came with his noblest noblemen, and the swindlers each raised an arm as if they were holding something. They said, "These are the trousers, here's the coat, and this is the mantle," naming each garment. "All of them are as light as a spider web. One would almost think he had nothing on, but that's what makes them so fine."

"Exactly," all the noblemen agreed, though they could see nothing, for there was nothing to see. "If Your Imperial Majesty will condescend to take your clothes off," said the swindlers, "we will help you on with your new ones here in front of the long mirror."

The Emperor undressed, and the swindlers pretended to put his new clothes on him, one garment after another. They took him around the waist and seemed to be fastening something—that was his train—as the Emperor turned round and round before the looking glass. "How well Your Majesty's new clothes look. Aren't they becoming!" He heard on all sides, "That pattern, so perfect! Those colors, so suitable! It is a magnificent outfit."

Then the minister of public processions announced: "Your Majesty's canopy is waiting outside." "Well, I'm supposed to be ready," the Emperor said, and turned again for one last look in the mirror. "It is a remarkable fit, isn't it?" He seemed to regard his costume with the greatest interest. The noblemen who were to carry his train stooped low and reached for the floor as if they were picking up his mantle. Then they pretended to lift and hold it high. They didn't dare admit they had nothing to hold.

So off went the Emperor in procession under his splendid canopy. Everyone in the streets and the windows said, "Oh, how fine are the Emperor's new clothes! Don't they fit him to perfection? And see his long train!" Nobody would confess that he couldn't see anything, for that would prove him either unfit for his position, or a fool. No costume the Emperor had worn before was ever such a complete success.

"But he hasn't got anything on," a little child said. "Did you ever hear such innocent prattle?" said his father. And one person whispered to another what the child had said, "He hasn't anything on. A child says he hasn't anything on." "But he hasn't got anything on!" the whole town cried out at last. The Emperor shivered, for he suspected they were right. But he thought, "This procession has got to go on." So he walked more proudly than ever, as his noblemen held high the train that wasn't there at all.

This fairy tale can be seen as a parable with a strong moral. It is *purposeful*. People should not succumb to social pressures which violate reality and one's own sense of *purpose*. Many things that are untrue are paraded as reality by people who do not want to seem out of touch with the prevailing world view, no matter how erroneous it is. Think of the totalitarian aspect of political correctness in today's world.

The riddle of Rumpelstiltskin and the parable of "The Emperor's New Clothes" are very different. The saving knowledge of the dwarf's name comes only by chance. The knowledge of the nudity of the emperor comes from a little boy who makes up his own mind and is not overwhelmed by social pressure.

The wide use of riddles and of riddling language in ancient Greek stories and writings, especially by oracles and prophets, is puzzling. Why don't they speak clearly? Why do their responses provoke a search for *meaning*? The gods themselves were unreliable, unpredictable, and even criminally vicious, certainly not a force for harmony and stability.

As we have argued in the previous chapter, the world itself, as Hesiod described it, began in *chaos*. Life is a riddle and the human being becomes obsessed with searching for its *meaning*. Chaos must be controlled if not completely subdued. The parable of "The Emperor's New Clothes" is *purposeful,* and its lesson is *purposeful* There is no need to search for *meaning*. The world according to Genesis begins in formlessness (*tohu vovohu*). But it is *purposeful. Tohu vovohu* must be shaped, but not controlled as with the Greek *chaos*. In the biblical view, God is a potter, not a jailor.

For the classicist E. R. Dodds, "Oedipus is a kind of symbol of the human intelligence which cannot rest until it has solved all the riddles—even the last riddle, to which the answer is that human happiness is built on an illusion."[5] Life is without inherent *purpose*. To the Greek thinker, life itself was a riddle, but not a pleasant one. One could not have real knowledge, nor is there any stability nor security.

In a sense, the world remains the *chaos* which Hesiod says it was at its beginning. No matter what one accomplished or gained in life, he could never let himself be happy, because tomorrow it might all be gone. This contrasts notably with the Bible's description of Abraham at the end of his life as being "satisfied with days." Life is a journey, a great parable. Man does not need to search for *meaning* in grand activities. Living *purposively* is sufficient.

How strongly the parable-riddle distinction characterizes the difference in Greek and biblical thought! The implications for contemporary education are significant. Consider the different conceptions of time presented in biblical and Greek writings in regard to two objective time events: 1) people age, and 2) there is day and night. These facts can be expressed in a boring rote manner, or they can be expressed poetically.

The two alternate versions of the sphinx's question to Oedipus express these realities in riddle form. The first question goes as follows: "Which creature has one voice and yet becomes four-footed and two-footed and three-footed?" Oedipus is reported to have answered: "Man, who crawls on all four as an infant, walks on two legs as an adult, and with the help of a cane as an elder." This "correct" answer to the riddle represents a cyclical curvilinear view of aging, and life itself; the old is like the young. Oedipus subdues the sphinx through answering its riddle but is "rewarded" for this by being wedded unknowingly to his mother, Jocasta, this incestuous coupling violating and indeed obliterating the line of demarcation between one generation and the next.

---

5. Dodds, *On Misunderstanding Oedipus.*

This view is dramatically different from that expressed in the Hebrew Bible, where the passage of time is not feared. The passing of the matriarch Sarah illustrates that each phase of life is appreciated on its own terms and is also expressed poetically and more in parable form. "And the life of Sarah was a hundred and seven and twenty years; these were the years of the life of Sarah."[6] Rather than simply stating that Sarah died at the age of 127, Genesis says that Sarah lived 100 years and 20 years and 7 years. The famous commentator Rashi states that she was as free from sin at 100 as she was at 20 (there is no liability for divine punishment until 20) and she was as beautiful at age 20 as at age 7.[7]

Consider now the second objective reality. Both day and night occur, and they alternate. This second version of the sphinx's riddle to Oedipus clearly expresses this view. "There are two sisters. One gives birth to the other, and she in turn gives birth to the first. Who are the two sisters?" Here Oedipus is reported to have answered: "Day and night, day giving birth to night, and then night giving birth to day."[8] Day and night are sisters, each replacing the other in an endless repetitive cycle. Although more poetic and creative, the message is that no growth or development occurs. It is the same story, day after day, night after night. It is the same old "same old."

Compare this to the description of the separation of evening and morning in Genesis 1: "And God saw the light, that it was good; and God divided the light from the darkness. And God called the light Day, and the darkness, he called Night. And there was evening, and there was morning, one day."[9]

Let us raise three questions. 1) What is the relationship of evening and morning? 2) Why not speak of night and day instead of evening and morning? 3) Why does the biblical day begin and end with evening? The sentence "And there was evening, and there was morning" appears at the end of each of the first six days of creation and is as poetic as the Greek riddle above. However, it provides a very different message. Life is not a cycle; day and night are not sisters. Rather, each day begins unformed and in darkness and emerges into light. Evening can be seen as the parent of morning, which then grows into evening. That evening then becomes parent to a new morning, not a recycling back to the first morning. This is not simply a

---

6. Gen 23:1.

7. Rashi on Gen 24:1.

8. Theodectes frag. 4, in Snell and Kannicht, eds., *Tragocorum Graecorum Fragmenta*, vol. 1.

9. Gen 1:4–5.

rote recitation of a boring fact,[10] but instead represents a parable of growth, and is radically different than the cyclical riddle that the sphinx poses to Oedipus. The book of Genesis begins with an account of God's creation of the world in six days. The first day ends with "And there was evening, and it was morning, one day."

Although the biblical account portrays the sun and moon as only created on the fourth day, God established an order of time and calendar from the very first day. The world he was creating would be harmonious and orderly, not chaotic. Day and night are not adversaries but are both parts of God's creation. Life represents not a *meaningless* cycle but *purposeful* development.

---

10. Again see Heiden, *Eavesdropping on Apollo*, 236–37.

3

Two Approaches to Life and Death

IN THIS CHAPTER, WE examine differential attitudes towards life and death as expressed in Greek tragedy and the Hebrew Scriptures. Characters in Greek tragedy are obsessed with a search for *meaning*. And *death* is the default. Figures in biblical stories, in contrast, are trying to *live* with *purpose*.

SUICIDES IN GREEK TRAGEDY

In a highly original work, Milton Faber[1] points to the prevalence of suicide by Greek figures in the tragedies of Sophocles and Euripides. Approximately sixteen suicides and self-mutilations can be found in the twenty-six surviving tragedies of Sophocles and Euripides. Only one suicide occurs in the seven surviving plays of the third great Greek tragedian, Aeschylus. One might object that this is cherry-picking; after all, we are speaking of "tragedies."

However, John Donne lists three pages of suicides occurring in historical figures in classical Greece and Rome in his iconic work *Biathanatos*.[2] The works of ancient biographers such as Plutarch and Diogenes Laertius

---

1. Faber, *Suicide and Greek Tragedy*.
2. Donne, *Biathanatos*.

recount many suicide tales: of Pythagoras, Socrates, Zeno the Stoic, Demosthenes, the statesman Marc Antony, the younger Seneca and his wife, Paulina, and many more. In addition, Graeco-Roman literature provides numerous examples of collective suicide in the ancient world, where men first slaughtered their families and then themselves.[3]

But let us concentrate here on the plays of Sophocles and Euripides to try to understand what was going on the Greek mind and how this was involved in a search for *meaning*. The great sociologist and founder of the discipline of suicidology, Emil Durkheim (1897–1951), distinguished three distinctive types of suicides: 1) egoistic suicides resulting from an isolation of self from society, 2) altruistic suicides resulting from a lack of differentiation between self and society and, 3) anomic suicides, referring to a confusion in boundaries between self and society. Most of Sophocles' depicted suicides are egoistic in this sense and are equally divided between men and women. Most of those in Euripides' tragedies are altruistic and all are women. Let us examine some of these suicides in terms of a search for meaning on the part of these protagonists. We are very indebted to the excellent work by the previously mentioned Milton Faber in this regard.

Table 1: Suicides in Greek Tragedies of Sophocles (S) and Euripides (E)

Character	Gender	Source	Method	Type
Ajax	Male	*Ajax* (S)	Sword	Egoistic
Deianeira	Female	*The Trachinae* (S)	Sword	Egoistic
Eurydice	Female	*Antigone* (S)	Knife	Egoistic
Haemon	Male	*Antigone* (S)	Sword	Egoistic
Jocasta	Female	*Oedipus Rex* (S)	Self-hanging	Egoistic
Oedipus	Male	*Oedipus Rex* (S)	Self-binding	Egoistic
Antigone	Female	*Antigone* (S)	Self-hanging	Anomic
Heracles	Male	*The Trachinae* (S)	Self-burning	Anomic
Hermione	Female	*Andromache* (E)	Suicidal threats	Anomic
Phaedra	Female	*Hippolytus* (E)	Self-hanging	Anomic
Alcestis	Female	*Alcestis* (E)	Self-poisoning	Altruistic
Evadne	Female	*The Suppliants* (E)	Self-burning	Altruistic
Iphigenia	Female	*Iphigenia in Aulis* (E)	Axe	Altruistic
Macaria	Female	*The Heracleidae* (E)	Knife	Altruistic
Menoeceus	Female	*The Phoenissae* (E)	Knife	Altruistic
Polyxena	Female	*Hecuba* (E)	Sword	Altruistic

3. Cohen, "Masada, Literature, Tradition," 385–405.

Oedipus the King (*Oedipus Rex*) contains one egoistic suicide (Jocasta) and one anomic self-mutilation (Oedipus himself). Jocasta hangs herself when the tragic truth of her incestuous relationship with her son Oedipus is revealed. Oedipus rushes into the palace determined to murder his mother-wife, Jocasta, but when he discovers that she has hung herself, he plunges the golden brooch she was wearing into his eyes, blinding himself.[4] Why do they do this?

Consider first Jocasta. Her sense of *purpose* as a wife of Oedipus and mother of their four children has come to a crashing halt with her realization that she is Oedipus's mother as well as his wife. She cannot tolerate this loss of *meaning* and exits this life. Oedipus's sense of *purpose* as a benevolent king and loving husband and father is also shattered by the realization he has murdered his father and bedded his mother. He is filled with shame so great that he cannot simply kill himself, because he may see his natural parents in *Acheron* (the next world). So he takes out his eyes in an attempt to hang on to some *meaning* structure that his act is shameful.[5] In fact, Oedipus was entrapped by the misleading answer of the Oracle, who told him he would kill his father and marry his mother without answering Oedipus's question as to the identity of his parents.[6]

Sophocles' *Antigone* contains three suicides: those of Antigone (anomic), Haemon (egoistic), and Eurydice (egoistic). Let us focus on Antigone, the daughter of the incestuous union of Oedipus and Jocasta, who has buried her rebel brother Polyneices against the order of her uncle Creon.[7] Creon responds by burying Antigone alive.[8] She hangs herself—mimicking the death of her mother. Her actions indicate a search for *meaning* in her death. Significantly, her name, *Anti-gone* in Greek, can be interpreted as denoting being "against generativity (or motherhood)."[9]

Two more suicides occur in Sophocles' *The Trachiniae*: the anomic self-stabbing of Deianeira, the grateful yet abandoned wife of Heracles, and Heracles' own egoistic self-burning on a pyre. Let us concentrate on Deianeira. Again we are indebted to Farber's analysis of her psychological makeup. When Deianeira learns Heracles has abandoned her for Iole, she sends Heracles a robe dipped in the blood of a centaur that Heracles had

---

4. Sophocles, *Oedipus the King*, ll. 1265–70.

5. In a modern trilogy of plays on Oedipus, I have raised the question of why Oedipus does not kill himself *after* taking out his eyes. After all, now blinded, Oedipus would not see his parents in Acheron (Kaplan, *Oedipus in Jerusalem*, *Oedipus Redeemed*, and *Oedipus the Teacher*).

6. Sophocles, *Oedipus the King* ll. 788–93.

7. Sophocles, *Antigone*, ll. 450–51.

8. Sophocles, *Antigone*, ll. 524–25.

9. Kaplan and Cantz, *Biblical Psychotherapy*, 168–69.

previously slain. On a conscious level, Deianera thinks this robe will serve as a charm to win her husband's love back to her. Unconsciously, the robe expresses her fury and perhaps a negative life meaning, by bursting into fire and sticking to Heracles' skin, causing him great agony, and ultimately his suicide. When Deianera realizes what she has done, she offers no expression of sympathy or remorse towards Heracles, but stabs herself in her own marriage bed, presumably the same bed Heracles intends to share with Iole.[10] This act seems to provide *meaning* for Deianera, but in a most perverse way. The mortally wounded Heracles, wracked in pain, enlists the aid of his son Hyllus to throw him onto a funeral pyre and, significantly, to marry his (Heracles') mistress, Iole.[11]

Perhaps the gold standard of an egoistic suicide is that of the great Greek warrior Ajax in Sophocles' play of the same name. Ajax has gone mad with jealousy because Achilles' armor, after his death, has been given to Odysseus rather than to him (Ajax). In a frenzied state, Ajax tries to murder Odysseus. The goddess Athena prevents him from doing so by deflecting his anger so that he slaughters a herd of sheep instead. The subsequent realization by Ajax of what he has done can be said to shatter his meaning structure as a great warrior. As Ajax's rage passes, it is replaced by a self-destructive depression emerging from his perceived lost honor in the eyes of his father. An honorable suicide becomes in his eyes his only solution, which will have the attendant benefit of receiving his mother's attention. This need appears in Ajax's daydream of her grief at his death: "She, woeful woman, when she hears these tidings will wail out a large dirge through the entire town."[12] Immediately after this refrain, Ajax falls on his sword and dies.

Suicides occur in seven of Euripides' surviving plays as well: *Hippolytus*, *The Phoenissae*, *The Suppliants*, *Alcestis*, *The Hericleidae*, *Hecuba*, and *Iphigenia in Aulis*. Most of these suicides are women, and fall into a pattern of ritual murder, in which the protagonist does not actually raise a hand against herself but allows herself to be sacrificed. Let us examine the role of the search for meaning in some of these suicides.

In *Hippolytus*, Phaedra, the wife of King Theseus of Athens, hangs herself after being caused, by the goddess Aphrodite's design, to fall madly in love with her misogynistic, vain, and moralistic stepson, Hippolytus. Though she resists her passion, with great misery to herself, her servant betrays her secret to Hippolytus.[13] Phaedra hangs herself, leaving behind a

10. Sophocles, *Trachiniae*, ll. 524–25.
11. Sophocles, *Trachiniae*, ll. 1221–78.
12. Sophocles, *Ajax*, ll. 848–49.
13. Euripides, *Hippolytus*, ll. 1354–60.

note that falsely accuses Hippolytus of raping her. Phaedra destroys herself because she is embedded in a miserable situation. Her suicide seems to provide some sort of saving meaning in her life.

In *Alcestis*, King Admetus of Thessaly is told that the fates demand his death unless he can find someone who is willing to die in his place. Admetus' aged parents sharply refuse his request, but Alcestis, his young and beautiful wife, kills herself in his place.[14] In the opening scene, the god (Death) meets Apollo in a deadly serious debate for the life of Alcestis. Humans do not really have a right to enjoy their life on the earth: who they are and what they have accomplished mean nothing. In the end, the netherworld makes demands that create a *meaning structure* that one of the characters must die. Alcestis bows to this *meaning structure* and satisfies Death's claims.

The Heracleidae begins after the death of Heracles. Afterwards, his family seeks refuge in Athens from his old enemy, King Eurystheus of Argos, who wishes to kill them. Demophon of Athens is willing to help the fugitives, but an oracle pronounces that a girl of noble descent must be sacrificed to the goddess Persephone in order for him to defeat the Argives. Heracles' daughter Macaria learns of the trouble from Iolaus, her father's old friend, and she seems to take total responsibility by offering herself as the victim. Iolaus is greatly moved by Macaria's altruistic gesture, praising her as a true daughter of Heracles. He suggests a fairer method, a lottery involving Macaria and her sisters, but Macaria will have none of this. It has no *meaning*. Her sacrifice for others has no *meaning* if it is imposed through a lottery. "My death shall no chance lot decide, there is no graciousness in that peace, old friend. But if ye accept and will avail you of my readiness, freely do I offer my life for those, and without constraint."[15]

Euripides' *Hecuba* describes the sacrifice of Polyxena, prisoner of the Greek conquerors after the fall of Troy and the last surviving daughter of Queen Hecuba and King Priam. The play commences with the Greek fleet ready to return home after sacking Troy. The ghost of Achilles appears and demands that a Trojan virgin be sacrificed on his tomb before the fleet can sail. The Greeks vote that the virgin to be sacrificed is Polyxena. What is so telling is her reaction. First, there is Polyxena's sense of shattered *meaning*: "For my own life, its ruin and its outrage, never a tear shed; nay death is become to me a happier lot than life."[16] Second is her insistence that her death is a heroic act, and indeed voluntary. Indeed, she prefers death to unheroic behavior. Rather than rebuke her executioners for murdering her,

---

14. Euripides, *Alcestis* 1.394.
15. Euripides, *Heracleidae*, ll. 541–43.
16. Euripides, *Hecuba*, ll. 210–11.

she seems to forgive them. Like Macaria, she seeks to create the illusion of control over her own death: "Of my free will I die; let none lay hand on me; for bravely will I yield my neck."[17] This insistence on her death being voluntary provides a *meaning* structure in her life.

Iphigenia in Aulis portrays Euripides' final suicide, that of Iphigenia, daughter of Agamemnon, which may be the most poignant and illustrative of all of Euripides' altruistic suicides. Iphigenia, following the pattern described above of Macaria and Polyxena, accepts willingly, almost gladly, a seer's order that she must be sacrificed before her father's army will be able to sail for Troy. This is the gold standard for ritual murder, not suicide in the contemporary use of the word. However, in this play there is no real distinction.

The play's characters are encumbered with the same problem as so many other characters of Greek drama—the general cheapness of human life in its heroic view of man. Agamemnon laments: "Woe's me for mortal men! None have been happy yet." All must go as the fates will.[18] Nevertheless, Agamemnon still feels compelled to kill Iphigenia, even when his brother Menelaus relents in his demands for her sacrifice. Indeed, Iphigenia herself seems to avoid any active attempt to evade her death. Rather, she grasps for a freedom that she does not really have by trying to make her death seem voluntary instead of obligatory: "I have chosen death: it is my own free choice. I have put cowardice away from me. Honor is mine now. O mother, say I am right."[19] It is this stance that give her essentially involuntary death as *meaningful*.[20]

A number of points stand out in these great but tragic Greek plays.

1. Life is ultimately tragic, with no hope of redemption. Heroic suicide and self-sacrifice offer a *meaning structure* not available in everyday life.
2. Greek figures are unable to develop a healthy view of themselves in society. People cannot really change, but only cycle back and forth between suicidal polarities. Either they are altruistic (e.g., Euripides' Iphigenia) or egoistic (Sophocles' Ajax), or both.
3. Protagonists are totally isolated from their surrounds (Ajax), or urged or even compelled to let themselves be sacrificed for a larger goal.

17. Euripides, *Hecuba*, ll. 559–62.
18. Euripides, *Iphigenia in Aulis*, ll. 442–45.
19. Euripides, *Iphigenia in Aulis*, ll. 1375–77.
20. Only one semi-overt act of self-destruction occurs in the seven surviving plays of Aeschylus, the third great Greek tragedian; specifically, in *The Seven Against Thebes*, where Eteocles, son of Oedipus and Jocasta, rushes to the battlefield, insisting the gods are eager for his death (ll. 692–719).

Some (e.g., Macaria, Polyxena and Iphigenia) attempt to convert an involuntary sentence imposed upon them into a voluntary exit.
4. There is no attempt to intervene to prevent characters (e.g., Ajax) from committing suicide. Ajax is left alone, without human company or any offer of simple comforts such as food or drink.
5. All these suicides and self-destructive behaviors seems to serve in their own distorted way, a *meaning*-making function otherwise missing in the characters' lives.[21]

SUICIDES IN THE HEBREW BIBLE

The biblical God puts life and death before human beings and they are commanded to choose life.

> I have set before thee today life and death, the blessing and the curse, therefore choose life that thou mayest live, thou and thy seed.[22]

While suicide is not directly forbidden in the Hebrew Scriptures, the Talmudic tradition sees suicide a most heinous sin and derives a prohibition from Noahide laws, applying to all people.

> And surely your blood of your lives will I require; at the hand of every beast will I require it; and of every man's brother will I require the life of man.[23]

---

21. Overall, there are approximately 246 characters who appear in the 26 plays of Sophocles and Euripides—many in more than one play.
    Approximately 16 suicides (including one self-mutilation) can be found in the 26 surviving tragedies of Sophocles and Euripides, including 12 by female characters. Eight instances of suicidal behavior (including one self-mutilation) can be found among the approximately 63 characters (exclusive of unspecified figures such as the Greek chorus) in the seven plays of Sophocles, yielding a suicide rate of 12.6 percent. Of these, four of the suicides occur among the 45 male characters depicted (8.8 percent), while the four remaining suicides occur among the 18 female characters depicted in Sophocles (22.2 percent). The gender difference in suicide is even more pronounced in the 19 surviving Euripidean plays. Here, approximately 173 characters are depicted, with no suicides occurring among the 123 male figures and eight among the 50 female characters (16.7 percent). Only one suicide, a male character, Eteocles, occurs in the seven surviving plays and 41 depicted characters of the third great Greek tragedian, Aeschylus. There are approximately 185 characters who appear in the 26 plays of Sophocles and Euripides—many in more than one play. Granted, these characters are fictional, but their depiction provides a portal into the way the Greek tragedians thought with regard to life and death.
22. Deut 30:19.
23. Gen 9:5.

Yet there in reality is little discussion of it. The emphasis instead is in daily life having inherent *meaning*. The minutiae in the laws of Sabbath observance or the laws of animal sacrifice in the temple occupy far more space in the literature. For example, in the eighth volume of the *Aruch HaShulchan*, only one page covers the subject of suicide (*Yorah Deah*, 345).[24]

Unlike the ancient Greeks, the biblical human being finds meaning in everyday life. Life meaning does not have to be searched for in grandiose adventures.

Nevertheless, six suicides (all male) are described in the Hebrew Bible, none in the Pentateuch. Chronologically, they are the self-stabbing of Abimelech,[25] the crushing of Samson,[26] the self-stabbing of Saul[27] and his armor-bearer,[28] the hanging of Ahitophel,[29] and the burning of Zimri.[30]

Table 2: Suicides in the Hebrew Bible

Character	Gender	Source	Method	Type
Saul	Male	1 Sam 31:4	Sword	Altruistic
		2 Sam 1:6		
		1 Chr 10:4		
Saul's armor-bearer	Male	1 Sam 31:5	Sword	Altruistic
		1 Chr 10:5		
Ahitophel	Male	2 Sam 17:23	Strangling	Egoistic
Zimri	Male	1 Kgs 16:18	Burning	Egoistic
Abimelech	Male	Judg 9:54	Sword	Egoistic
Samson	Male	Judg 16:30	Crushing	Altruistic

24. This statement has been seen as a prohibition not only against suicide but also against any form of self-mutilation (*Baba Kamma*, 91b). The Hebrew Bible contains several additional prohibitions regarding self-mutilation, for example: "Ye are the children of the Lord your God: Ye shall not cut yourselves, nor make any baldness between your eyes for the dead" (Deut 14:1). Much the same prohibition is given specifically to the priests in Leviticus: "They shall not make baldness upon their head, neither shall they shave off the corners of their beard, nor make any cuttings in their flesh" (Lev 21:5).

25. Judg 9:54.

26. Judg 16:30.

27. 1 Sam 31:14; 2 Sam 1:6; 1 Chr 10:4.

28. 1 Sam 31:15; 1 Chr 10:5.

29. 2 Sam 17:23.

30. 1 Kgs 16:18.

Ahitophel, a counselor of King David, has joined Absalom's rebellion against David. But when he perceives that Absalom has been tricked into following a foolhardy plan that is certain to lead to David's victory, it seems that Ahitophel's *meaning* structure has been shattered. In response, Ahitophel sets his house in order and strangles himself.[31] Several reasons, all egoistic, have probably prompted Ahitophel's suicide. First, he fears that Absalom's attempt to overthrow David is doomed and that he will die a traitor's death. Second, and less likely, is Ahitophel's disgust at Absalom's conduct in setting aside his counsel, which has wounded Ahitophel's pride and disappointed his ambition. Rabbinic writers have also argued that, since Ahitophel is a suicide, his family inherits his estate. If he were to be executed as a rebel, his possessions would be forfeited to the king. So his suicide may serve a meaning function in terms of taking care of his descendants.

Zimri is also an egoistic suicide. King Elah of Israel passes his days drinking in his palace while his warriors battle the Philistines. Zimri, a high-ranking officer, takes advantage of this situation, assassinates Elah, and mounts the throne. His reign, however, lasts only seven days. As soon as the news of King Elah's murder reaches the army on the battlefield, they pronounce General Omri to be king and lay siege to the palace. When Zimri sees that he is unable to hold out against the siege, his *meaning* structure seems to shatter and he sets fire to the palace and perishes in the flames: "And it came to pass, when Zimri saw that the city was taken that he went into the castle of the king's house, and burnt the king's house over him with fire, and he died."[32]

Abimelech's suicide is, strictly speaking, an assisted suicide. After carving out a principality for himself in Israel by means of various brutalities, he is mortally wounded by a millstone that a woman throws from a fortress she is besieging. Realizing that he is dying, Abimelech asks his armor-bearer to finish him off so that it will not be said that a woman has killed him. This represents a *meaning* structure, as distasteful as it may be, and classifies as an egoistic suicide.[33]

Now we come to three more sympathetic biblical suicides: Samson, Saul, and Saul's armor-bearer. Samson, the great defender and leader of the Israelites, had been blinded and publicly mocked by the Philistines. Faced with torture and death, he asked God for the strength to take as many Philistines with him as possible; when granted his request, he

---

31. 2 Sam 17:23.
32. 1 Kgs 16:18.
33. Judg 9:53–57.

pulled down the central pillars of the temple of Dagon, killing thousands in one last blow:

> Strengthen me, I pray, just this once . . . And Samson took hold of the two middle pillars which supported the temple, and braced himself against them, one on his right and the other on his left. Then Samson said, "Let me die with the Philistines.[34]

It is tempting to see Samson as the biblical equivalent of Sophocles' Ajax. Samson, like Ajax, has fallen from his previous state of leadership. Is he too using suicide to restore his lost image in the eyes of others? Closer examination indicates that Samson's suicide is not egoistic like that of Ajax: he is not alienated from his society but is very much a part of the people of Israel. Is Samson's suicide, therefore, altruistic and self-sacrificing? We must also reject this interpretation. Samson does not suffer from a failing sense of his own personality; rather, he calls on God to strengthen him in his final attempt to destroy the Philistines. His *purpose* is not self-annihilation but the carrying out of his divinely ordained mission to free Israel from the Philistines. Samson's suicide thus seems to be neither egoistic nor altruistic; rather, it may be labeled covenantal in the sense that it is in the service of his God, and thus has *meaning* in this sense. Significantly, his final action in life leads to a long period of peace.[35]

A second covenantal suicide is that of King Saul. Rabbinic literature has regarded King Saul as a man of great stature, the anointed of the Lord. Yet his reign was marked by series of mistakes, ending with his own suicide during a losing battle against the Philistines on Mount Gilboa. Saul has seen three of his sons and many of his fighters slain, and he himself is severely wounded. Surrounded by enemies and not wishing to be taken prisoner and exposed to the mockery and brutality of the Philistines, King Saul entreats his armor-bearer to kill him. The latter refuses and Saul falls on his own sword: "Then Saul said to his armor-bearer: 'Draw your sword, and thrust me through with it, lest these uncircumcised men come and thrust me through and abuse me.' But his armor-bearer would not, for he was greatly afraid. Therefore, Saul took a sword, and fell on it."[36]

The suicide of Saul has been taken by commentators in different ways. The *Midrash Rabbah*[37] has pointed to Saul as an example of a permissible suicide. One commentator has considered Saul as a special case because,

---

34. Judg 16:28–30.
35. Judg 13.
36. 1 Sam 31:4.
37. Midrash Rabbah on Gen 9:5; 34:3, and Shulchan Aruch, Yoreh Deah, 345.3.

before the final battle with the Philistines, he has received a message from the witch of Endor that he will die. Thus, by taking his own life, he is not defying providence. Other commentators have viewed Saul as an example of a suicide who takes his own life in order to avoid greater profanation of the divine name. In this view, Saul fears that if he is captured alive by the Philistines, they will desecrate his body, either by torture or by forcing him to commit idolatrous acts.[38]

SUICIDE PREVENTION IN THE HEBREW BIBLE

Perhaps even more to the point are six suicide-preventing, indeed life-promoting narratives described in the Hebrew Scriptures.

Table 3: Suicide Preventions in the Hebrew Bible			
Character	Gender	Source	Method
Rebecca	Female	Gen 27–28	Appropriate Matchmaking
Moses	Male	Num 11	Support and practical advice
Elijah	Male	1 Kgs 18–19	Protected withdrawal and nurturance
Jonah	Male	Jonah	Protected withdrawal and guidance
David	Male	Ps 22	Renewal of faith in God
Job	Male	Job	Renewal of relationship

Let us start with the story of the prophet Elijah. As a result of his prophetic denouncement of Queen Jezebel, she sends Elijah a messenger announcing that she intends to have him killed.[39] Elijah flees for his life into the wilderness and sits down under a broom tree, and he requests that he might die,

---

38. Some 2,855 different people (2,730 men and 125 women) are mentioned in the 39 books of the Hebrew Scriptures, spanning a period of some 3,330 years. Only six are identified as completed suicides (see Table 2 below), yielding an overall suicide rate of 6/2855 or .02 percent, including none by women. If we limit our estimate of the total number of biblical characters to the 1,778 identified by one title or another, such as king queen, prophet, judge military commander, etc. (Ziffer, *All the People of the Bible*), the suicide rate increases slightly to 6/1778 or .03 percent. Both of these rates are extremely significantly lower than the suicide rates emerging in Greek tragedy described above, whether we compare them to the sixteen suicides (6.8 percent suicide rate) for the 236 characters who appear in the 26 plays of Sophocles and Euripides (Chi-Squares = 133.13 and 80.03, p's<.0001 in both cases) or to the 6.1 percent suicide rate for the 277 characters when we include the seven plays of Aeschylus (Chi-Squares = 121.69 and 72.84, p's <.0001 in both cases).

39. 1 Kgs 19:1–2.

saying: "It is enough; now, O Lord, take away my life; for I am not better than my fathers." Elijah is at the end of his rope and says he cannot go on.[40] God is portrayed as listening to his prophet Elijah and taking his statement to heart and sends an angel to him. Elijah lies down and sleeps under a broom tree, and an angel touches him and says to him:

> "arise and eat": and he looked, and behold, there was at his head a cake baked on the hot stones, and a cruse of water. And he did eat and drink and laid him down again. And the angel of the Lord came again the second time, and touched him, and said: "Arise and eat; because the journey is too great for thee." And he did eat and drink, and laid him down again and he arose, and did eat and drink, and went in the strength of that meal forty days and forty nights unto Horeb the mount of God.[41]

Moses expresses suicidal wishes to God when he feels overwhelmed by his burdens which he feels he must shoulder alone: "I am not able to bear all these people myself alone because it is too heavy for me."[42] And then challenging, indeed imploring God to kill him, Moses cries out: "If thou deal thus with me, kill me, I pray Thee, out of hand, if I have found favor in Thy sight; and let me look upon my wretchedness."[43] God responds and provides him with the help of seventy people, a Sanhedrin, to share Moses' burden:

> And the Lord said unto Moses: Gather unto Me seventy men of the elders of Israel, whom thou knowest to be the elders of the people, and officers over them; and bring them unto the tent of meeting, that they may stand there with thee. And I will come down and speak with thee there: and I will take of the spirit which is upon thee, and will put it upon them, and they shall bear the burden of the people with thee, that thou bear it not thyself alone.[44]

The story of Jonah begins with God calling on him to go to Nineveh warn the people there of their wickedness. Jonah does not want to go, but he is too God-fearing to defy the command. In despair he boards a ship to flee to Tarshish, and hides from God in the innermost part of the ship and falls deeply asleep. However, God sends a great storm after Jonah and the ship is in danger of being broken apart and capsizing.

40. 1 Kgs 19:3–4.
41. 1 Kgs 19:5–8.
42. Num 11:14.
43. Num 11:15.
44. Num 11:16–17.

Jonah's shipmates cast lots to determine the cause of the storm, and the lot falls on Jonah. Only now, upon being questioned, does Jonah reveal his identity as a Hebrew, and admits that he has fled from the Lord. And only now, in response to his shipmates' questioning of how to bring calm, does Jonah advise them to throw him overboard to bring calm, which they do.[45]

The story could thus end in Jonah's suicide, but it doesn't—God intervenes as a protective parent, swallowing Jonah in the protective stomach of a great fish until he overcomes his confusion. Jonah prays to God from the belly of the fish until he becomes stronger. Unlike Narcissus, he comes to "know himself." Then the fish vomits him out on dry land.[46]

This same pattern repeats itself. God again asks Jonah to go to Nineveh. This time Jonah goes and gives the people God's message. They repent and are saved.[47] Jonah becomes angry and again expresses the wish to die and leaves the city to sit on its outskirts.[48] Again, God intervenes, sheltering Jonah with a leafy bush from the burning sun.[49] After a worm destroys the protective bush, Jonah once again expresses suicidal thought.[50] This sets the stage for God engaging Jonah in a mature dialogue to teach him the message of *teshuvah*—repentance or return—and divine mercy, and that he can reach out to another without losing himself.[51]

The story of the biblical matriarch Rebecca is more familial in scope. After participating in the deception by which they obtain Isaac's blessing, Rebecca sends Jacob away to his uncle Laban so that he won't be killed by an angry Esau.[52] Immediately afterward, Rebecca tells Isaac that "she has become weary of her life because of the behavior of her son Esau's Hittite wives, and she worries that Jacob may marry similarly.[53] Rebecca's words seem more like a message of despair to her husband. Isaac listens to his wife and commands Jacob to go to Rebecca's kinsman Laban and marry one of his daughters. Rebecca is relieved, and there is no more talk of suicide.

Deeply disappointed about the complaints of the Israelites, Moses cries out to God that the responsibilities of leading the people are too great and that God should kill him:

45. Jonah 1:1–12.
46. Jonah 2.
47. Jonah 3:1–10.
48. Jonah 4:1–3.
49. Jonah 4:6.
50. Jonah 4:7–8.
51. Jonah 4:9–11.
52. Gen 27:42–45.
53. Gen 27:46.

> So Moses said to the Lord, "Why have You afflicted Your servant? And why have I not found favor in your sight, that you have laid the burden of all these people on me? . . . I am not able to bear all these people alone, because the burden is too heavy for me. If You treat me like this, please kill me here and now—if I have found favor in Your sight—and do not let me see my wretchedness!"[54]

God, the divine therapist, does listen and intervenes with a positive and practical solution. Let Moses select seventy elders to help him lead the Israelites.[55]

The book of Job is one of the most challenging in the entire Hebrew Bible. We will compare the story of Job to Zeno in the next chapter. Let us summarize it here with regard to God's role in preventing Job's suicide. A just man, Job is assailed by a series of awesome misfortunes: the loss of his wealth, his family, and his health. Further his friends turn against him, questioning his innocence,[56] and even his wife urges him to "curse God and die."[57] Job rebukes her, saying: "What, shall we receive good at the hand of God, and shall we not receive evil?"[58]

Job is deeply grieved by these events, but his existential faith in God and life is not destroyed. Job does express what a modern suicidologist might interpret as a threat of suicide: "So that my soul chooseth strangling and death rather than these my bones. I loathe it; I shall not live always. Let me alone; for my days are vanity."[59] Still, what Job is really interested in is a reaffirmation of his relationship with God.

Job maintains his innocence in his suffering,[60] refusing to be silent,[61] and again he expresses the weariness of his life while he calls on God for *meaning*: "My soul is weary of my life."[62] Even so, he again refuses to be silent: "I will say to God, 'Do not condemn me; show me why You contend with me.'"[63] Job finds strength in his faith: "Though He slay me, yet will I

---

54. Num 11:11–15.
55. Num 11:16–19.
56. Job 2:11–31.
57. Job 2:9.
58. Job 2:10.
59. Job 7:15–16.
60. Job 9:21.
61. Job 10:1.
62. Job 10:1.
63. Job 10:2.

trust Him."[64] Indeed, he will continue to trust God no matter what God does to him. He asks only that God maintain an open relationship with him: "Then call, and I will answer; me speak, then You respond to me."[65] Beginning in Job 38, God does speak directly to Job, confirming the importance of their continuing relationship and God's care for his creation. Even though Job cannot understand God's ways, God continues his love for him. And this sense of being loved even through misfortune sustains Job.[66] We will return to Job in the next chapter, comparing him to Zeno the Stoic with regard to searching for *meaning*.

David too exhibits despair, abandonment, and even suicidal thoughts in some of his psalms, but the psalmist renews his faith in God and overcomes these feelings of heavy self-doubt. An example of this process can be seen in the famous Psalm 22. It begins in despair over the psalmist's perception of his complete and utter abandonment by God.

> My God, my God, why have You forsaken me?
> Why are You so far from helping me, and from the words of my groaning?
> O My God, I cry in the daytime, but You do not hear . . .[67]

Indeed, the first verse of this psalm is cited in the Gospel of Matthew as the last words Jesus utters as he is dying on the cross.[68] Psalm 22 continues with the psalmist's return to the roots of his faith—to the earliest stages of trust.[69] He overcomes the reproach of mockers and recovers his faith and thus overcomes his despair.

> But You are He who took me out of the womb;
> You made me trust while on my mother's breasts.
> I was cast upon You from birth,
> From my mother's womb You have been my God.[70]

God provides the stopper. He has been the rock of the psalmist's faith since the primal experiences of birth and nursing. This basic trust that the psalmist has established with God is sufficient to overcome the writer's doubts and fears of abandonment:

---

64. Job 13:15.
65. Job 13:22.
66. Job 38f.
67. Ps 22:1–3.
68. Matt 27:46.
69. Erikson, *Identity, Youth and Crisis*.
70. Ps 22:9–11.

Nor has He hidden His face from him.
But when he cried to Him, He heard.[71]

The following four summary points stand out in these biblical narratives.

1. Life is ultimately hopeful, with an intrinsic sense of *purpose*. Heroic suicide and self-sacrifice are not necessary to provide *meaning* in life. Being human is enough.
2. Biblical figures, both men and women, are able to develop a healthy view of themselves in society. People can and do change. They are encouraged to be themselves within the context of relationships with others. They truly develop rather than cycle back and forth. When they reach a temporary dead end, help is available to help them restore their strength and move ahead.
3. Characters under attack are able to fight back and remain defiant. They do not have to convert an involuntary assault against them into the illusion that it is voluntary
4. There is an attempt to keep others from ending their lives (e.g., Elijah). This gesture does not have to be grand but often involves providing simple comforts such as food or drink and the opportunity to rest.

Only one suicide, Judas Iscariot appears in the Christian New Testament either by hanging (Matthew 27:5) or falling and bursting open (Acts 1:18). Other suicides have been reported in the non-rabbinic writings of the Second Temple period as well. In the apocryphal book of 1 Maccabees, for example, Eleazar sacrifices himself by darting beneath the elephant of an enemy general and running his sword into it (1 Macc. 6:46). In the book o 2 Maccabees, two acts of suicide are recorded: first, that of Ptolemy, and second, that of Ragesh (Razis). Ptolemy, an advocate of the Judeans at the Syrian Court of King Antiochus Eupator, poisons himself after being accused of treason (2 Macc. 10:12). Ragesh first attempts unsuccessfully to die on his sword rather than fall into the hands of the Syrians (2 Macc. 14:41-42). He subsequently succeeds in disemboweling himself after throwing himself from a wall (2 Macc. 14:43-46). The historian Flavius Josephus also mentions a number of suicides in his work Wars of the Jews, including the mass suicides at Jotapata in 69 C. E. and Masada in 73 C.E.) (see the surveys of biblical suicides of Koch, 2005 and Shemesh, 2009).

It is incorrect to claim that there are no suicides in biblical and later Jewish history. Individual suicides have occurred despite the injunctions against them. Nevertheless, suicide is strongly prohibited in biblical and later Jewish thought, and when it has appeared within the culture, it may

71. Ps 22:24.

represent individual idiosyncrasies, impossible external situations, or profound Greco-Roman influences. The basic Jewish preference for life over death as expressed in the Hebrew Bible has never changed, nor has suicide ever been idealized as an end in itself. No Talmudic passage can be taken as praising suicide or glorifying heroism in the Greek sense, nor is there an obsession with death as the solution to life's problems or with the issue of control. Nevertheless, according to the Talmud, suicide can be permissible and even preferred in select instances in which a person is faced with forced apostasy or tortures that might be more horrifying than death.[72]

72. The great scholar Rabbi Hanina ben Teradion, who was burned to death by his Roman persecutors with a Torah scroll wrapped around him, would not even open his mouth so as to breathe in the flames and die more quickly: "Let him who gave me my soul take it away but no one should injure himself." In other words, he refused to advance his own death actively. The Roman executioner, impressed by the personal greatness of Rabbi Hanina and the terrible awe of the moment, wanted to be joined to him (Tosefot Avodah Zarah, 18a; Maharsha). He offered to end Hanina's torture by removing the wet sponges from around his heart, which had artificially prolonged his life. Rabbi Hanina approved this, and he assured the executioner of a portion in the world to come. 5 The executioner then removed the sponges, and, knowing that he himself would now be severely punished by the Romans, he leaped into the fire. Both were assigned a place in the world to come (Avoda (Avodah Zarah, 18a; Sifre and Yalkut Shimoni on Deut. 32:4).

The story of the 400 boys and girls who leaped into the sea rather than be sent to lives of prostitution in Rome is comparable (Gittin, 57b). There is a similar story in Lamentations Rabbah, 1.45, where the basic principle is that if "they feared lest idol worshippers force them to sin by means of unbearable tortures, then it is commanded to destroy oneself " (Tosafot, Avodah Zarah, 18a; Gittin, 57b; see also Rabbi Jacob Emden, Hagahot). At such a point it may be more desirable to sanctify God's holy name by suicide than to sin. Again, this is not an approbation of suicide per se, nor an obsession with issues of control, as in many of the Greek suicides. Human life remains an object of great importance. We should note that the young people in Gittin 57 and the elders in the parallel story in Lamentations Rabbah asked for a rabbinic opinion before leaping into the sea, so that they would not lose their share in the world to come. Gittin also describes the suicide of Hannah after the martyrdom of her seven sons, and Avodah Zarah 18b recounts the suicide of Beruria, the wife of Rabbi Meier.

Other Talmudic suicides include the Hasmonean princess who was loved by her former slave, Herod (Baba Batra, 3b), a Roman officer who saved the life after the father threw their son from the roof for receiving food from a guest without permission (Hullin, 94a). Another suicide involved a student whose name was falsely besmirched by a prostitute (Berachot, 23a). The Talmud (Semachot, chaps. 2 and 5) also relates two incidents of childhood suicide, the first involving the son of Gornos of Lydda, who ran away from school, and the second, that of a child in Bnei B'rak, who broke a bottle on the Sabbath. Each child killed himself after his father threatened to punish him; neither was ruled an intentional suicide. Two more suicides are mentioned in the Midrash Rabbah. The first (Ecclesiastes Rabbah 10:7) describes a pagan eunuch of the emperor of Rome who attempted to embarrass Rabbi Akiba. When the eunuch was shamed in return, he killed himself. The second (Genesis Rabbah 65:22) describes the suicide of Jakum of Tzeroth who, after taunting Rabbi Joseph Meshitha, inflicted as self-punishment the four modes of execution typically sentenced by the courts: he stoned, burned, strangled, and decapitated himself.

There are a number of significant suicides in later Jewish history as well, including five hundred Jews at York in the twelfth century, hundreds in Verdun, France, in 1326, and many more in response to the Spanish Inquisition. While it is not our intention to create a laundry list here, there have been periods of external persecutions throughout Jewish history that have put Jews in the position of choosing apostasy or suicide (Haberman1946). Durkheim's aforementioned observation on the comparatively higher rate of suicide among Jews in late nineteenth-century Bavaria and the suicides among Jews in Central and Eastern Europe in the 1930s and during World War II are also clearly connected to external forces. The importance of the theme of suicide in modern Yiddish literature has been explored in a work by Janet Hadda (1988), who has focused largely on suicidogenic family themes.

Famous Jewish suicides in modern times include that of Otto Weininger, the self-hating Jewish intellectual who in 1903 shot himself in Ludwig van Beethoven's apartment; Ernst Toller, a playwright and revolutionary who killed himself in New York in 1939 in despair after the fall of Madrid to Francisco Franco; and Samuel Zygelbojm, who in 1943 committed suicide in London to protest the in difference of Polish, British, and other authorities to reports of the Holocaust and the savage destruction of the Warsaw Ghetto. According to some accounts, Sigmund Freud, who was suffering from a painful and incurable illness, also took his own life.

4

Job against Zeno

Living Purposively versus Dying in a Search for Meaning

ZENO THE STOIC

Let us leave Greek tragedy and turn to the problematic narrative of the death of Zeno the Stoic (Zeno of Citium), the founder of the Greek school of Stoicism, as recorded in *The Lives of Eminent Philosophers* by Diogenes Laertius. Zeno of Citium taught in Athens from about 300 BCE on. Diogenes Laertius is not necessarily regarded as a serious historian but more as recorder of historical anecdotes and pieces of information. Here is what Laertius says about the death of Zeno.

> The manner of his (Zeno's) death was as follows. As he was leaving the school he tripped and broke his toe. Striking the ground with his fist, he quoted the line from Niobic, "I come, I come, why thou calls for me?" and died on the spot through holding his breath.[1]

The reader probably is asking several questions at this point. First, "Why in the world does Zeno kill himself over such a minor mishap?" Secondly, "What is the method he chooses to do it? Is it even medically possible?"

---

1. Diogenes Laertius, *Lives of the Eminent Philosophers* 7.28.

Let us address the first question first. Why does Zeno stubbing his toe lead to his taking his life? Diogenes Laertius is clear on this point. Zeno interprets his wrenching his toe as a sign from the gods that he should depart. This is objectively such a minor mishap that it is difficult to comprehend Zeno's motivation. There is no doubt that suffering great misfortune, or even continuing small setbacks, can create feelings of despair that some people seem to be able to overcome, while others cannot. But this is not the case here. Zeno is portrayed as taking his life after the relatively minor mishap of stubbing (perhaps breaking) his toe. He is aging, and perhaps alone, ill, or just gerophobic, but he seems almost to be looking for a sign that he should exit his life. He is searching for *meaning*. Zeno's student Cleanthes takes his life in a very similar fashion. Initially he fasted to cure a boil on his gum. But he refused to stop fasting even when the gum boil was cured.[2]

Even more curious is the method Diogenes Laertius tells us Zeno uses to kill himself. *He holds his breath until he dies*. We certainly have encountered examples of people putting closed bags over their head as a means of suffocating themselves. Bruno Bettelheim's sad ending is an example of this.[3] But let us emphasize that Bettelheim asphyxiated himself by putting his head in a closed bag, not by holding his breath.

However, this is not how Zeno's death is described. There is no bag! Zeno is portrayed as *holding his breath until he dies*. But this is medically impossible. Breathing is involuntary and if a person holds his breath, he will become unconscious, and then begin to breathe again. So what is going on here? Why is this the description of Zeno's death. In a search for *meaning*, the biological fact that breathing is involuntary is violated. Zeno "holding his breath" until death defies the biological reality with regard to the involuntary aspect of breathing, and to the biblical conception that God breathes life into man and takes it away.[4]

Some writers cite Zeno's actions as a precedent for rational suicide. However, they may not be focusing on what is rational in Zeno's act. Zeno's rationality lies not in his interpretation that stubbing his toe represents a sign from the gods that he should depart, but rather in his need for the events in his life to have *meaning*. Zeno is aging and feels alone. His life *purpose* seems to be gone, and he deludes himself into thinking that the act of stubbing his toe has cosmic *meaning*. Zeus cares enough about him to send him a sign. Zeno wants to remain significant, even if he dies in the process. Its *rationality* is not that stubbing his toe is a sign to depart, but that

2. Diogenes Laertius, *Lives of the Eminent Philosophers* 7.176.
3. Goleman, "Bruno Bettelheim Dies at 86."
4. Gen 2:7.

it is better to have a world in which one's actions are given *meaning*, even destructive meaning, than one in which they are not. But this begs the question: Why is Zeno looking outside his own life to find *meaning*? Where is his life *purpose*? Is it not provided by his Stoic philosophy? Is Zeno's search for *meaning* at heart a desperate attempt on the part of Zeno to deny the facticity of his actual human condition? It seems narcissistic to the extreme, and almost laughable if it was not so deadly. And let us not forget that Narcissus himself is described as a suicide by both Ovid[5] and Conon.[6]

THE BIBLICAL JOB

We have discussed the biblical story of Job is very different. In contrast to Zeno, Job does not commit suicide despite being assailed by far more serious misfortunes—the loss of his wealth, his family, and his health. He is not obsessed with a search for meaning and does not catastrophize.

Job's friends tell him to admit he deserves his punishment, but he refuses because he knows it is not true.[7] He certainly complains bitterly but does not break his relationship with God. On the opposite extreme, his wife tells him to "curse God and die."[8] But he rejects this response as well. Job is deeply grieved and indeed wrestles with suicide, indeed stressing the same method of death, *strangling*, as did Zeno. "So that my soul chooseth strangling, and death, rather than these bones."[9] Strikingly, however, he differs from Zeno in not seeing breathing as a voluntary act. Further, he is not overwhelmed by the calamities befalling him, continuously reaffirming his relationship with his Creator. "Though He slay me, yet will I trust in Him."[10]

Job, in contrast to Zeno, is anchored in a sense of a personal Creator who is with him from the moment of his birth and will be with him into his death and beyond. This sense gives him a natural sense of *purpose*, so that he does not have to "search for *meaning*." Thus, he can withstand far greater misfortunes than can Zeno without the need to attribute cosmic *meaning* to them. This does not make Job less rational, but simply anchors his interpretive structure in his purposeful desire to live. Job follows the biblical injunction that one is born against one's will, and dies against one's

5. Ovid, *Metamorphoses* 3.497–502.
6. Ovid, *Narrationes* 24.
7. Job 4–32.
8. Job 2:9.
9. Job 7:15.
10. Job 13:15. Exline et al., "Anger, Exit and Assertion" points to the importance of being able to argue within a relationship with God without leaving it.

will, and expresses his freedom in the way he lives his life.[11] Thou renews the face of the earth."[12]

In contradistinction to Zeno, who is improbably described as "holding his breath until he dies," the book of Job stresses that it is God himself that has given Job the breath of life. "The spirit of God hath made me, and the breath of the Almighty giveth me life."[13] If he withdraws that breath, man returns to the dust from which he sprung. "Thou withdrawest their breath they perish and return to their dust."[14] And when God restores the breath, man rises again and renews the face of the earth. "Thou sendest forth Thy spirit, they are created."

It is telling that the Hebrew Scriptures specifically warn against us against looking for such signs. It specifically forbids consulting necromancers or fortune-tellers.[15] He overcomes major losses in his life by deepening his faith in his Creator, who provides him with an inherent *purpose* for his life.

Job's three "friends"—Eliphaz, Bildad, and Zophar—come to visit Job and tell him that he deserves what has befallen him.[16] If Job is afflicted in this way, then he must have sinned. But Job maintains his sense of innocence and sarcastically unmasks his friends' pretensions of superior wisdom,[17] referring to them as "miserable comforters,"[18] and questions the morality of God's "justice." He simply does not comprehend it and will not pretend to understand something that he cannot understand. As the story proceeds, God appears in a whirlwind, describing himself as an unquestionable power. Yet God punishes Job's three friends for presuming to say they understand his ways and instructing them to offer burnt offerings to his servant Job, who shall pray for them.[19] Then he turns to Job and tells him that he (Job) alone has spoken the truth, that God's ways are not understandable to human beings. God himself is rejecting the notion that he is bound by a simple-minded "just world hypothesis" and acquiescing to the sense that, on the surface, the world may not appear to be a just and orderly

---

11. Job 4:29.
12. Ps 104:30.
13. Job 33:4.
14. Ps 104:29.
15. Lev 19:3; 20:6; Deut 18:9–12.
16. The tendency to see the world as an invariably just place.
17. Job 12.
18. Job 16:2.
19. Job 42:7–9.

place where people always get what they deserve.[20] Yet at the same time, life has inherent *meaning*, even in the worst of situations. One does not need to search for it.

Only when Job accepts this more elevated conception of God does he become restored twofold, in everything. God, in fact, asks Job to pray for his doubting friends, which he does, and Job names his first daughter Yemima, meaning "dove" and deriving from the Hebrew word *yom*, meaning "day."[21]

This is a very interesting response with double-edged implications. On the one hand, God's response represents a strong rebuke to the friends of Job, who continually accuse Job of guilty behavior leading to his afflictions. On the other, God is rebuking Job himself for demanding tit-for-tat accountability. In other words, his afflictions are no indicator that he has sinned, nor does his just and righteous behavior ensure that he won't suffer afflictions. Let us reiterate, this is the polarity of a simple-minded "just world hypothesis" in which the world is a just and orderly place where people always get what they deserve.[22] Under this view, if one suffers, one deserves it. Rather, God is communicating that his ways are beyond human understanding. When Job accepts this more elevated conception of God, he becomes restored.

Job does not need to continuously search for such *meaning* through catastrophizing and overinterpreting relatively minor misfortunes. Job's God gives and takes away life but does not give signals that it is time for Job to depart. Job is not obsessed with death, nor does he need to control it, nor does he need to worry that it is timely. Job thus does not interpret each event as a signal to exit, but as a challenge to live the life that has been given to him in dignity. Life for Job has inherent *purpose*, and this represents the best alternative and antidote to the obsession of death with dignity and rational suicide so endemic to Zeno the Stoic and contemporary culture. Job, in contrast, is anchored in a sense of a personal Creator who is with him from the moment of his birth and will be with him into his death and beyond.

Job does not understand why these calamities are happening to him, nor does he pretend to understand it, as do his friends. Job does not overinterpret each event as a signal to exit, as does Zeno the Stoic, but as a challenge to live the life that has been given to him in dignity. Life for Job has inherent *purpose*, and this represents the best alternative and antidote to the obsessive search for *meaning* that can be so destructive in contemporary life. We summarize these respective life stories below as a point of contrast.

20. Lerner and Miller, "Just World Hypothesis."
21. Job 42:9–17.
22. Lerner and Miller, "Just World Hypothesis."

Table 4: Job against Zeno		
Stage	Zeno the Stoic	Job
1. Precipitating stressor	Zeno trips and stubs a toe on the way back from lecturing at the stoa.	Job suddenly and unexpectedly loses his property, his children, and his health.
2. Reaction	Zeno seems to be obsessed with finding *meaning* behind his mishap and interprets his minor injury as a sign from the gods he should depart.	Though Job complains, he maintains his innocence and his sense of *purpose* despite the calamities that have befallen him. He has an inherent *purpose* and needs not search for *meaning*. He rejects his friends' view that he is guilty and his wife's that "he should curse God and die."
3. Response of others	No mention is made of the reaction of others	Job's three friends tell him that he must be guilty. His wife tells him to curse God and die.
4. Effect	Zeno immediately holds his breath until he dies.	Job maintains his faith in God while proclaiming his innocence. God punishes Job's friends for saying they understand his (God's) ways and tells Job that he alone has spoken the truth and restores him.

5

Purpose versus Meaning

in Biblical and Stoic Thought

LET US LEAVE THE specific comparison of Zeno and Job ask if Zeno's death is representative of Stoic philosophy, which is generally seen as a view reasonable people may see as an alternative to religious belief. And it seems to have replaced a biblical approach to life for many modern intelligent people. It is usually seen as guide to forbearance and patience enduring life's travails. Stoicism is generally admired as a sober, serious philosophy, quite removed from Greek tragedy and its many suicides we have discussed earlier in chapter 2. Yet, close analysis of Zeno's death in chapter 4 suggests Zeno's death is not so benign. We wish to explore here if Zeno's death represents an outlier or if it is part and parcel of the Stoic philosophy.

WHAT DID THE STOICS BELIEVE?

The Stoics seemed to regard neither life nor death as very important. At the same time, they seemed almost obsessed with the idea of suicide as a way of overcoming their fear of death. In a sense, the Stoics attempted to conquer death by choosing it on their own terms. At best, the philosopher should commit suicide not to escape suffering but to avoid restrictions in carrying out life, since he should be as unaffected by suffering as by any other emotions. A central problem prompting the Stoic view of life was a pervasive fear of a loss of control—ultimately, control over life itself. For the Stoics, cheerfulness was a philosophical duty, not an indication of any natural positive emotion or optimism, or any inherent love of life. This suggests a tendency to interpret life stressors as a way to justify exiting life (i.e., suiciding). They did not seem to be filled with any hope deriving from a underlying sense of *purpose.*

Zeno, defined the goal of life as living in agreement with nature.[1] If such an agreement exists, life is good; if it does not exist, suicide becomes the wise choice.[2] Therefore, as we have discussed in the previous chapter, Zeno was said to have killed himself out of sheer irritation (perhaps because of imperfection itself) when he wrenched his toe by stumbling on his way home from the stoa. He held his breath until he died.[3] His successor, Cleanthes, fasted to death. Initially, he fasted to cure a boil on his gum. However, "he had advanced so far on his journey toward death, he would not retreat," and he starved himself to death.[4]

The Roman Stoics basically agreed with their earlier Greek counterparts—with one important shift. The question was no longer whether to kill oneself when the inner compulsion became irresistible, but how to do so in the right way.[5] This attribute can be seen in a sampling of the writings of Cicero.

> Suicide, Cicero argues, is no great evil. When a man's circumstances contain a preponderance of things in accordance with nature, it is appropriate for him to remain alive: when he possesses or sees in prospect a majority of the contrary things, it is appropriate for the wise man to quit life, although he is happy, and also for the foolish man to remain in life although he is miserable . . . And very often it is appropriate for the wise man to abandon life at a moment when he is enjoying supreme happiness, if an opportunity offers for making a timely exit. For the Stoic view is that happiness, which means life in harmony with nature, is a matter of seizing the right moment. So that Wisdom, her very self, upon occasion bids the wise man to leave her. According to Cicero, "appropriate" means "in accordance with nature, as is self-love"; thus, suicide is useful to the wise man.[6]

1. Diogenes Laertius 7.87
2. Diogenes Laertius 7.130.
3. Diogenes Laertius 7.130.
4. Diogenes Laertius 7.176.
5. Alvarez, *Savage God*, 62.
6. Cicero, *De Finibus* 3, ll. 60–61.

In the *Tusculan Disputations*, Cicero depicts death as freeing humans from chains. The gods in their benevolence have prepared for humans a haven and refuge after their departure from worldly life.[7] Some philosophers disagreed with this, and some Stoics may even feel that the soul is not immortal. Indeed, while earthly life is not wholly evil, the afterlife holds far more joy.[8]

Cicero cites the deaths of Socrates and Cato as examples that suicide is permissible, but only when the gods themselves have given a valid reason. One must not break the prison bonds except in obedience to the magistrate. The human soul should be dissociated from the body during life by means of philosophy and virtue, for such a life will best prepare the soul for the afterlife. It is highly desirable for one to quit the sorrows of this world to gain the joys of the next.[9]

Much the same view can be seen in a sampling of the declamations of Seneca the Elder (ca. 40 CE). These declamations were a series of arguments on a variety of subjects and were widely used as training for law students. Whatever may have been the various opinions in individual cases, it is clear that suicide was hardly shocking to either the speakers or the listeners.

The Stoic seems to feel bound by necessity and seeks a sense of freedom and release. In this area, among others, the philosophy of Stoicism seems to suffer from a sort of constipation. In one of the clearest statements of Stoicism, Cicero fears a loss of control, even to the point of life itself. He argues that suicide is inappropriate when a man's circumstances are positive and appropriate when they are negative,[10] and depicts death as freeing man from chains.[11] Chains? Life is a prison? Is this what Stoics believe?

The younger Seneca puts it this way: One should escape from this life whenever he chooses, and he should die when the means are at hand: "Choose any part of nature and tell it to let you out."[12] One should pick the means by which to quit life, for the option of suicide leaves the road to freedom open. To grumble is pointless, since life holds no one fast. "Do you like life? Then live on. Do you dislike it? Then you're free to return to the place you came from."[13] The philosopher may choose his own mode

---

7. Cicero, *Tusculan Disputations* l.18
8. Cicero, *Tusculan Disputations* 1.84.
9. Cicero, *Tusculan Disputations* 1.71–75
10. Cicero, *De Finibus Bonorum et Malorum* 3.60
11. Cicero, *Tusculan Disputations* 1.18, 84.
12. Seneca, *Epistles*, 117.23–24.
13. Seneca, *Epistles* 70.15.

of death just as he chooses a ship or a house. He leaves life as he would a banquet—when it is time.[14]

In one of the clearest statements of Stoicism, the Roman Cicero argues that suicide is inappropriate when a man's circumstances are positive and appropriate when they are negative.[15] In the latter case, Cicero depicts death as freeing man from chains.[16]

Hmm. This does not read much like a life-affirming philosophy. Do other stoics view life the same way? Let us return to Seneca. He continues this line of thinking, specifically equating suicide with freedom.

> You see that yawning precipice? It leads to liberty. You see that flood, that river, that well? Liberty houses within them. You see that stunted, parched and sorry tree? From each branch, liberty hangs. Your neck, your throat, your heart are so many ways of escape from slavery . . . Do you inquire the road to freedom? You shall find it in every vein of your body.[17]

Philosophical talk can be easy, but does Seneca really put this philosophy into action? To put it more prosaically: He talks the talk, but does he walk the walk? The answer is *yes*! Seneca and his wife Paulina put their thoughts into action, methodically cutting their wrists in a tub of hot water while drinking wine, albeit at the order of Seneca's former pupil, the emperor Nero. Why does such a seemingly reasonable philosophy lead to suicide?

The Stoic sees fate or *moira* as a powerful force capriciously controlling human destinies. The chains of necessity were so strong that they desperately sought to escape them. If heroic gestures would not suffice, then suicide would. In particular, the Stoics tried to escape from the inevitability of death through the illusion of gaining control over death through suicide. Knowing that he could bring about his death by slitting his wrists gives Seneca the "feeling of freedom in every vein." The option of bringing about his death seemed to give the Stoic an illusion of control by which he could prevent death from striking him by chance. Let us be blunt. The possibility of suicide seems to give the Stoic an escape from the *meaninglessness* of life. We are forced to conclude that Zeno's death by suicide does not represent an outlier with regard to Stoic philosophy and is part and parcel of the emptiness of the Greek view of life and its attendant search for *meaning* in signs, which we have been discussing.

14. Seneca, *Epistles* 70.11; Plotinus, *On Suicide* 1.9.
15. Cicero, *De Finibus Bonorum et Malorum* 3.60.
16. Cicero, *Tusculan Disputations* 1.18, 84.
17. Seneca, *De Ira* 3.15.3–4.

Droge and Tabor[18] cite Zeno's actions as a precedent for rational suicide. However, they may not be focusing on what is rational in Zeno's act. *Zeno's rationality lies not in his interpretation that stubbing his toe represents a sign from the gods that he should depart, but rather in his need for the events in his life to have meaning.* Zeno is aging and feels alone and deludes himself into thinking that the act of stubbing his toe has cosmic meaning. Zeus cares enough about him to send him a sign. Zeno becomes a hero, even if he dies in the process. Its inherent rationality is not that stubbing his toe is a sign to depart, but that it is better to have a world in which one's actions are given *meaning*, even destructive meaning, than one in which they are not. This view is narcissistic to the extreme, and quite deadly. And let us reemphasize our earlier observation that Narcissus himself is described as a suicide by both Ovid[19] and Conon.[20]

So then, is Zeno's search for *meaning* at heart a desperate attempt to deny the facticity of his real human condition? Camus is even more pessimistic, arguing that all lives are equally *meaningless* because of the inevitability of death. Because all humans will eventually die, all lives are equally *meaningless*.

WHAT DOES BIBLICAL THOUGHT BELIEVE?

It is telling that the Hebrew Scriptures specifically warn against us looking for *meaning* to fill an empty place in one's being. It specifically forbids consulting necromancers, soothsayers, and fortune-tellers.[21] Both Jewish and Christian Scripture assert that life has inherent *purpose* and there is no need to obsessively search for *meaning*.

Let us begin with a quote from Genesis:

> And God said, Let us make man in our image, after our likeness: and let them have dominion over the fish of the sea, and over the fowl of the air, and over the cattle, and over all the earth, and over every creeping thing that creepeth upon the earth.[22]

This passage states clearly that the human being has an inherent *purpose*: to tend to God's creation. Since God created man in his image, man's *purpose* cannot be fulfilled apart from him. This passage both places

---

18. Droge and Tabor, *Noble Death*, 29–39.
19. Ovid, *Metamorphoses* 3.497–502.
20. Conon, *Narrationes* 24.
21. Lev 19:3; 20:6; Deut 18:9–12.
22. Gen 1:26–27.

structure on human beings and sets limits on acceptable behavior. It is *purposeful* to care for the earth and its inhabitants and unacceptable to be destructive towards it. Yet the earth is not made into a god and worshiped or alternatively violated as in the Greek and Roman worlds. We will return to this issue in greater detail in a subsequent chapter.

A passage in Exodus restates the *purposeful* nature of life. God has a *purpose* for everyone.

> But I have raised you up for this very purpose, that I might show you my power and that my name might be proclaimed in all the earth."[23]

The *purposeful* nature of life is stated again in the first book of Samuel. We find *purpose* by serving God. "We fulfill our purpose of glorifying God also by living our lives in relationship and faithful service to Him."[24]

The book of Ecclesiastes tells us that King Solomon tried to find *meaning* in his life by living hedonistically for his own pleasure. Yet at the end of his life he concluded that they were mere vanities. "Vanity of vanities, saith Koheleth, all is vanity"[25]; the only worthwhile life is a *purposeful* life, one of honor and obedience to God.

> The end of the matter, all having been heard; fear God, and keep His commandments; for this is the whole man. For God shall bring every work into the judgment concerning every hidden thing, whether it be good or whether it be evil.[26]

Yet these plans are not simply boilerplate documents for everyone. Each person is uniquely created in God's image and thus has been given a unique *purpose* to his life.

> For Thou has made my reins.
> Thou hast knit me together in my mother's womb.
> I will give thanks unto Thee, for I am fearfully and wonderfully made . . .[27]

God has a unique plan and *purpose* for each of us.

How different these lines ring from the ending of *Oedipus the King* by Sophocles.

---

23. Exod 9:16.
24. 1 Sam 12:24.
25. Eccl 12:8.
26. Eccl 12:13–14.
27. Ps 139:13–16.

> Therefore while our eyes wait to see the destined final day, we must call no one happy who is of the mortal race, until he hath crossed life's border, free from pain.[28]

Let us repeat the statement of Camus that the only certain thing in life is the inevitability of death, and because all humans will eventually die, all lives are equally *meaningless*.[29]

---

28. Sophocles, *Oedipus the King*, ll. 1528–30.
29. Camus, *Stranger*.

6

Two Clinical Cases

THIS CHAPTER WILL DISCUSS how our analysis of the contrast between Stoicism and biblical thought played out in two clinical cases I have been involved with. The names of the two patients have been disguised. In each case, the patient seemed to exhibit a *Zeno syndrome*. In each case, I attempted a *Job intervention*. One was successful, and one unfortunately failed. Let us present the failure first.

CASE 1: THE COMPLETED SUICIDE OF PATIENT CHARLOTTE

Charlotte's History

Let me describe the case of an eighty-one-year-old woman named Charlotte (name disguised), who had recently undergone a hysterectomy.[1] During the winter of 1996, the *Detroit Free Press* was conducting a "psychological autopsy" of the first forty-seven physician-assisted suicides performed by Dr. Jack Kevorkian. This involved interviewing friends, family, and health

---

1. Kaplan, "Martha Wichorek's Death"; Kaplan and Cantz, *Biblical Psychotherapy*, 117–23.

professionals who had interacted with the deceased in an attempt to develop a psychological profile of the deceased akin to a "physical medical autopsy." They approached me to be a psychological consultant on their study, and I gladly agreed. I had written a great deal on this topic and in addition was teaching a graduate course on suicide and suicide prevention in the psychology department at Wayne State University in Detroit, where I was a professor. I mention this to show that I was a semipublic figure on the topic of suicide during this period.

On December 2, 1996, I received a copy of a letter from a person I did not know. It turned out to be the first of many letters and was written in impeccably neat, perhaps computerized, handwriting. It was hand-addressed to me at the beginning and with her signature at the end. I discovered that a good number of public figures in the psychological, medical, legal, and political realms received this and subsequent letters. In this letter, Charlotte argued strongly for the legalization of euthanasia clinics in Michigan. Her letter read as follows.

> Dear Friend
>
> In matters pertaining to the euthanasia-assisted suicide issue, we have heard and read a thousand times that "Only God gives life and only He should take it away." True, God does give life and also takes it away gradually, by way of old age, disease, drugs, etc.
>
> When "life" (being able to do things for yourself and others) is taken away, unless a heart attack or accident strikes first, every human being usually descends into the "miserable existence" stage (cannot do anything for yourself or others—totally helpless). This stage of that life-death cycle can last weeks, months or years and is the most dreaded of human experiences.
>
> We also hear and read "the sanctity of life," "concern for human life," "we must protect life," etc. Everyone agrees that it is right, moral and proper to sanctify, protect and value "life." However, when "life" is taken away and we Elderly, terminally ill, Alzheimer's, etc. descend into the "miserable existence" stage, very few officials and medical personnel acknowledge that this stage is a special stage and should receive special treatment. In fact, many just say "if the heart is beating, then the patient is alive."
>
> This refusal to divide the "life"–"miserable existence"–death cycle into distinct categories is causing most of the animosity in

euthanasia discussions. Many deliberately use the word "life" when they know very well that they mean "miserable existence."[2]

Charlotte continued for three full pages, stressing the suffering of people who were in a "miserable existence stage," which she also labelled the "other death row." She advocated for a state approved euthanasia clinic. She described a number of indignities of this "miserable existence stage": 1) a nursing home or hospital tests and procedures, 2) living with children, 3) hospice, 4) in-home and visiting nurse arrangements, 5) living wills, and 6) committing suicide without the help of a doctor. She signed the letter, "a still clear thinking 81-year-old human being."

In March 1997, I received another letter. The tone had darkened. Charlotte began to write of her own death and of using the money she would save through her death to buy her grandson (who was graduating from college) a car.

In April 1997, something new happened. I received another letter from Charlotte, this time from a hospital where she had undergone a hysterectomy after bouts with vaginal bleeding. She was doing fine and acknowledged that "she was getting stronger" but described the "torture" she was enduring. She specified: 1) "IVs with anesthetics, nutrients, etc."; 2) "tight rubber stockings that stretched from my toes to the crotch, and expanding and contracting legging attached to a motor for better blood circulation"; 3) "tubes in my nose, for oxygen"; 4) "breathing tubes to exercise my lungs"; 5) "blood pressure and temperature checks every hour, an EKG, blood drawn for lab tests, etc."; and 6) "I was expected to walk alone from the bathroom, holding onto the IV pole one day after surgery."

Anyone who has undergone surgery recognizes the "tortures" that Charlotte had described as unpleasant and temporary, but quite necessary, to help facilitate a quick recovery. Charlotte's comments indicated that she did realize the reason why these measures were taken. Yet she seemed to regard each of them as an assault on her dignity; further, that these assaults made "life not worth living." What was going on with Charlotte? She seemed to be behaving exactly like Zeno the Stoic. Was she looking for *meaning* in the same destructive way he was? Why could she not tolerate these minor indignities?

Charlotte went on to claim that in the absence of legalized euthanasia, she chose surgery "because the alternatives . . . such as living with children, in a nursing home, with hospice or home care arrangements were worse." What the heck was this all about? How could she be saying something so seemingly nonsensical? What was Charlotte searching for?

2. Kaplan and Leonhardi, Kevorkian, "Martha Wichorek and Us," 268.

Charlotte spent three days in the hospital. Her surgery, minor throughout, was successful and she returned home. I subsequently called her several times unsuccessfully over the nest period. No one answered the phone. I received no more letters during this next period and spent the summer months away from Michigan. I returned in September 1997 and was not successful in reaching her. I received no more letters from her.

On December 3, 1997, the newspapers, television, and radio in the Detroit area reported that Jack Kevorkian had assisted yet another person to take her life in Oakland County, Michigan. The name reported was Charlotte X, and she was the seventieth case identified as having been aided to die by Kevorkian.

The autopsy revealed the late Charlotte had no anatomical evidence of disease. She had stated elsewhere that she was not in pain, other than some mild age-related arthritis. The medical examiner of Oakland County, Michigan, confirmed to me that he could find nothing anatomically wrong with Charlotte in her autopsy. People who knew her said she had been active in her church in its fall cleanup. She had raked leaves, helped in painting a basement, and seemed to be in a generally cheerful mood. Why then did Charlotte kill herself?

Charlotte seemed to exemplify the aforementioned Zeno the Stoic, sadly hoping to find in her suicide a *meaning* to her life. As we mentioned in the previous chapter, Droge and Tabor may be correct in citing Zeno's actions as a precedent for rational suicide. However, as we argued, they may not be focusing on what is rational in Zeno's act. *Zeno's (and Charlotte's) rationality lies not in his interpretation that stubbing his toe represents a sign from the gods that he should depart, but rather in his need for the events in his life to have meaning.* Zeno is aging and feels alone and deludes himself into thinking that the act of stubbing his toe has cosmic *meaning*. Zeno becomes a hero, even if he dies in the process. Its inherent rationality is not that stubbing his toe is a sign to depart, but that it is better to have a world in which one's actions are given *meaning*, even destructive meaning, than one in which they are not. Charlotte behaved similarly. She was aging and felt alone and attempted to turn her death into a heroic martyrdom for the cause of euthanasia.

My Failed Job Intervention with Charlotte

I had tried to find a way of helping Charlotte find a *purpose* to her life. In retrospect, I realized that I had attempted almost unconsciously to employ the narrative of Job in my attempt to dissuade Charlotte from taking her life.

To recapitulate, I was concerned after receiving Charlotte's initial December 2, 1996, letter presented above. I contacted her by telephone and did an initial intake, though she was not my patient. Our conversation revealed that Charlotte had lost her husband to cancer three years previously and was the mother of three grown daughters. She lived alone and, aside from some normal ailments associated with aging, was in reasonably good health. She was not terminal, nor was she in acute physical pain. In fact, she seemed to be active in her community, had written three books, and had a very sharp mind.

Yet, as mentioned above, Charlotte advocated forcefully for a state-sanctioned clinic for "we terminally ill, Alzheimer's." Significantly, she was neither terminally ill nor suffering from Alzheimer's, and by her own description "still clear thinking." Nevertheless, Charlotte insisted she wanted to die before she became incapacitated or terminally ill. After speaking with her, I did not think that Charlotte was acutely suicidal at this moment. I was concerned, however, that her perception of her situation would tend to lead to a more concrete suicide. Further, I was worried that she presented such constricted thinking. I invited her to come to my university (Wayne State University) to talk with me. However, she refused, politely.

When I received Charlotte's March 1997 letter, I immediately contacted her by phone. I stressed the hostility underlying committing suicide to save money to enable her grandson to buy a car. I focused on the ambivalent feelings that her grandson would have assuredly toward a gift brought about by his grandmother's suicide. At this time, Charlotte told me about the death of her husband a few years previously. I acknowledged her loneliness and suggested she get involved in activities or even therapy. She rejected both of these options. I then emphasized Charlotte's capabilities and how much she had to offer in the fight for better healthcare for the elderly.

I invited Charlotte to present her views in the class I was teaching on suicide. Charlotte declined but said she enjoyed our calls. I suggested that she go see a psychologist or a counselor to talk about her situation. She refused again politely; I offered to come visit her. Again she declined, but gave me the phone number of a speakers bureau dealing with "problems of the elderly." Curious, I called the number. It was the law firm of Geoffrey Feiger, the lead attorney for Jack Kevorkian! Charlotte's legal knowledge and interests began to make some sense. Concerned, I resolved to keep in regular contact with her, though she was not my patient.

After receiving her April 1997 letter, both my colleague and I tried to see Charlotte. Again we were rebuffed, politely. I subsequently called her several times unsuccessfully over the nest period. No one answered the phone. I received no more letters during this next period and was away from Michigan over the summer months. I returned in September and was not successful in reaching her. I received no more letters from her.

On December 3, 1997, the newspapers, television and radio reported that Jack Kevorkian had assisted yet another person to commit suicide in Oakland County, Michigan (a very wealthy county just north of Detroit). The name reported was Charlotte X, and she was the seventieth case identified as having been aided to die by Kevorkian. When I heard her name, I personally felt as if I had been kicked in the head and resolved to investigate the case. Although Charlotte had not been my patient, I felt as if I had lost her. I wanted to know why she was so obsessed with wanting to die.

I did not need to wait long. That afternoon, I and others on her list received a neat suicide note from Charlotte insisting that she was rational and competent at the time of her death. "I am not stressed, oppressed, or depressed." She said. "I don't have Alzheimer's and am not terminally ill, but I am 82 years old and I want to die."

Again, the medical autopsy indicated that Charlotte had displayed no anatomical evidence of disease. She had stated elsewhere that she was not in pain, other than having some mild age-related arthritis. Let me reemphasize that the medical examiner confirmed to me that he could find nothing anatomically wrong with Charlotte in his autopsy.

People who knew her said she had been active in her church in its fall cleanup. She had raked leaves, helped in painting a basement, and seemed to be in a generally cheerful mood. Why then did Charlotte kill herself, and what does this teach us about "rational suicide"? Why did my attempts fail so completely?

The key to Charlotte's logic can be found in the definition of life she offered in her first letter to me, from December 2, 1996. To refresh our memories, let us state Charlotte's reasoning in terms of premises and conclusions.

1. "Life" (quotation marks hers) is being able to do things for yourself and others.
2. When this independence and self-sufficiency is taken away, every human being descends into the "miserable existence stage" (cannot do anything for yourself or others—totally helpless).
3. This "miserable existence stage" is a middle stage between "life" and death, which can last weeks, months, or years and is the most dreaded of human experiences.
4. Since this "miserable existence stage" is *not* "life," "euthanasia" of someone in this stage is "special treatment" and not "murder."[3]

---

3. Significantly, this definitional scheme of life applies to everyone, whether or not they might agree with it.

This argument is eminently logical and rational in the narrow sense of the term. First of all, life is defined in terms of independence and self-sufficiency and productivity. Second, and ominously, the taking away of this independence does not just make one feel "miserable," but actually puts one into another, morally and legally unprotected, "category": the stage of "miserable existence." The difference between being a living person who feels miserable and being no longer a living person, but one who has entered a "miserable existence" category, is monumental. The first category requires compassion. The second category requires "special treatment," a term which sends chills down the spine of anyone even remotely knowledgeable about the Nazi euthanasia program known as *T4*. This "special treatment" ends in the euthanasia of the person in this "miserable existence stage," whether he wants it or not.[4]

But why did I fail so completely fail in addressing Charlotte's misery? Why was I not able to implant in Charlotte any of the resilience so prominent in Job's life story? Why was I not able to demonstrate to Charlotte—really, to reach Charlotte with—the counternarrative implicit and explicit in the Job story? Why was Charlotte so focused on finding *meaning* in her death? What could I have done differently? Why was her search for *meaning* so focused on her death, and not on life?

We need to explore the psychological reasons behind Charlotte's decision to kill herself. A number of general suicidal themes stand out in Charlotte's letters. They are:

1. black-and-white negative thinking;
2. a counterphobic stance toward dependency (rejection of all help or assistance);
3. insistence on a nonbiological definition of life (as being able to take care of oneself);
4. use of euphemisms (she created a new life stage, "miserable existence," rather than describing herself as feeling miserable);
5. unsolicited speaking for others (she advocated for a state-sanctioned euthanasia clinic for "*we* terminally ill, elderly, Alzheimer's," even though she personally fell into none of these categories);
6. an overly rational, legalistic analysis of the problem of euthanasia and doctor-assisted suicide;
7. exaggeration of annoying but relatively minor and temporary discomforts;
8. an irrational tunnel vision behind her seemingly logical arguments;

---

4. Lifton, *Nazi Doctors*; Mitchell, "Of Euphemisms and Euthanasia."

9. an apparent blurring of her personal situation with the campaign to legalize euthanasia and the eagerness to make herself a martyr for the cause;
10. her plan to kill herself and to give her grandson a car with medication money she was saving;
11. reluctance to accept family support (she found death preferable to living with her children);
12. her choice to die (and be in control) rather than accept her current relatively healthy though somewhat diminished state.[5]

I have been long plagued by the question of how to have better employed the biblical story of Job to help her. Charlotte was not formally religious, yet she was most likely aware of this story. Desituated from its theological context, the story of Job is one of a man who does not commit suicide despite being assailed by far more serious misfortunes. First, Job is stuck by the loss of his great wealth and then the deaths of all his children. He reaffirms his faith in God.

Job knew that his God had created him uniquely in an act of living kindness. Why didn't Charlotte? Job knew his God gives and takes away life but does not give signals that it is time for him to depart because of any imperfection or disability. Why didn't Charlotte know this? Job did not focus on his "quality of life." Why did Charlotte?

Job did not focus on any particular attributes that make life worth living or not. Indeed, this is not even a question that seems to have occurred to Job. Why did it occur to Charlotte? Job was not obsessed with death, nor did he need to control it, nor did he need to worry if it was timely. Why was Charlotte? Job thus did not need to interpret each event as a signal to exit, in a fruitless attempt to find *meaning*—in the heroic. Why did Charlotte? Job simply needed to live the life that had been given to him in dignity and die when it was his time to die, without wild overinterpretation. Why didn't Charlotte? Job was not obsessed with death, nor did he need to control it, nor did he need to insist that it was timely. Why did Charlotte? Job thus did

---

5. This case also raised broader issues for me. 1) With legislation permitting assisted suicide and euthanasia, there is more chance for abuse (both by the financially driven choices in healthcare and also by families who wish their loved ones dead); 2) the extension of choice of assisted suicide to physically sound but depressed individuals; 3) the "quick" solution of death for the elderly when they feel useless (is there any relation between the rising rates of elderly suicide and the publicity related to assisted suicide and euthanasia?); 4) the substitution of "death with dignity" for "meaning of life"; 5) the focus of death as a *right* rather than as a *fact*, and the over-concern with the legal as opposed to the psychological and spiritual issues. The last point is worth reflecting on. The decriminalization of suicide in contemporary society does not mean that healthcare professionals should encourage it and not try to prevent it.

not interpret each event as a signal to exit, but as a challenge to live the life that had been given to him in dignity. Why did Charlotte? In short, why did she act like Zeno the Stoic in searching for *meaning* behind every single act?

Though Charlotte was not my patient per se, she had reached out to me and I was unable, as much as I tried, to meet with her and attempt to devalorize her idealized conception of suicide. I thought I knew how to apply what we now call the Job intervention, but she did not make herself available, and I lost her to totally unwarranted physician-assisted suicide. Had she been my patient, I would have focused on Charlotte's cognitive and emotional state and philosophical assumptions. I would have tried to change her worldview, to Hebraicize her, employing the narrative of Job and emphasizing that it is perfectly legitimate to complain about her life without leaving it.

Imagine you are psychotherapist or a religious counselor. How would you describe Charlotte?

A. Rational
B. Gerophobic: afraid of aging
C. Delusional: does not see things clearly
D. B and C

Secondly, how would you treat her, and how would you have employed the story of Job in your therapeutic approach had you had a chance to treat her? What would have been your Job Intervention?

A. Empathize with her about her ailments and loneliness, without exaggerating them.
B. Explore why she feels her ailments are a sign that she should depart.
C. Explore what is the basic *purpose* of her life.
D. All of the above.

My Life Lesson

We end the discussion of Charlotte with an explication of the following life lesson. We must emphasize an unassailable, inherent positive *purpose* to a depressed person who has been assaulted by misfortune. With this *purposiveness*, one is better able to feel of inherent worth and thus can withstand the tendency to catastrophize a misfortune into an often-melodramatic tragedy, overinterpreting events in a compulsive search for *meaning*. Without such an inherent life *purpose*, a person may exaggerate, personalize, and dramatize his misfortune in an attempt to find *meaning*, even with lethal consequences. Charlotte found *meaning* only in her death (as a release from life) and became a poster child for physician-assisted suicide. She behaved like an ancient Greek Stoic, indeed like Zeno himself. Her very search for *meaning* led her to take her own life. Her search for *meaning* was suicidal.

CASE 2: THE UNSUCCESSFUL SUICIDE ATTEMPT AND RECOVERY OF PATIENT HARRY

Harry's History

At the time he entered therapy with me, Harry, an osteopath in his late sixties who owned a chain of nursing homes, was going through a bankruptcy and a bitter divorce. He came in highly agitated and suicidal. He reported being depressed, but actually was also quite angry and aggressive. He had threatened legal authorities who had been coming after him and was generally very antagonistic. He needed to have the last word with regard to everything.

As therapy began, Harry reported he had been raised during the Depression (the 1930s) by a rejecting and ineffective father for whom he had no respect. He reported feeling that his father resented him for succeeding in school and was terrified that Harry would surpass him, and constantly undercut him. Harry reported his mother as ineffective in keeping his father from belittling him.

Harry reported being a self-made man who had done everything on his own. He had practiced as a physician in Michigan for a number of years and married a girlfriend from his college days whom he reported feeling was "totally ineffective" like his mother. She gave birth to three children. Harry was very dissatisfied with his marriage and could not wait for his children to leave the family home so he could file for divorce. And so he did during a period in which he was doing very well financially. He had opened up a chain of nursing homes, as mentioned above, and married a considerably younger woman (Roberta) who was working for him at one of his homes. Harry was flying high, made a good deal of money, and accrued considerable power. He was subsequently nominated to head an important county-level health department in southeastern Michigan. Yet Harry felt he was really alone and did not know whom to trust.

Now Harry was charged with the allegations that he had violated a number of requirements regarding poor staffing and unsanitary conditions at a nursing home. Many of his friends, including some with considerable influence, offered to help Harry but he rejected all their help, and accused them of siding with his enemies. Rather than attempt to achieve some conciliatory resolution with the prosecutors, he dug in his heals, and made matters worse rather than compromise, leading to his losing his homes and filing for bankruptcy. His appointment to the county position was also scuttled on the grounds that he was not responsible in handling his personal business affairs and could or would not follow basic health standards.

He became angry and abusive and drove his second wife, Roberta, away when she tried to help him. Roberta reacted bitterly and wrote him a letter, which he showed me, in which she blamed him for being dishonest with her before they were first married and highly manipulative. In this letter, she reported telling him she wanted children, and accused him of undergoing a vasectomy without telling her in advance while they were still dating. Harry admitted that this was true, because he was determined not to have any more children. He had already had three in his first marriage. When he did tell her he had undergone the vasectomy, she decided to marry him anyhow, but Harry felt she carried a resentment into the marriage. Specifically, Harry complained that Roberta spent more time with her sister's children than she did with him, which Harry became intensely jealous about. Harry told me that he felt Roberta was more married to her sister than to him. She said she "wanted out" because he was making impossible demands on her.

Shortly after entering treatment, Harry first threatened and then attempted suicide by overdosing, but survived. When he was released from the hospital, he brought in a letter from his son Richard, from his first marriage, also a doctor, from whom he was at least partially estranged. His son seemed to question the sincerity of his attempt. Specifically, Richard's letter contained the phrase, "your suicide attempt, if it was one."

Harry seemed more indignant than hurt over this note and insisted to me that he was a doctor and that he had taken enough pills "to kill three people." Puckishly, I asked: "Which three people were you trying to kill?" He responded immediately the names of three people that had led to the charges of violation of nursing home standards. I too had my doubts that his attempt was a full suicide attempt rather than a parasuicidal gesture. He was a doctor himself and in all likelihood knew how many pills to swallow to leave a trace in his blood and yet not run the risk of death or serious complications. Yet medicine is inexact, and people can and do die from parasuicidal gestures.

Harry's problem seemed to be that he was always on his own. Like Oedipus, he felt rejected by his own father and was never was able to trust anyone. He had to keep all his doubts to himself, and through a false bravado appear stronger and more completely self-reliant than he needed to be or indeed could be.

My Successful Job Intervention with Harry

My therapeutic intervention with Harry began with my trying to impress on Harry the impossibility of doing everything on his own. I impressed on him that he was making impossible demands on Roberta, and that he might be able to repair his relationship with her by realizing how badly he had hurt her with the lack of trust he had exhibited to her. He approached Roberta but she was not very receptive. I suggested they take a trip together and they decided to drive together to New Mexico. However, this plan did not work out very well, the blame not all on Harry's part. On the one hand, Roberta complained that Harry was imposing his itinerary on the trip. On the other hand, Harry reported that Roberta had showed no sign of taking any initiative for the trip. The trip ended with Roberta flying back home leaving Harry to drive their car back alone. This seemed to be the last straw for both, and Roberta filed for divorce.

Harry was furious and decided to swear off relationships. I pointed out to Harry that his very domineering attitude had inhibited Roberta from helping arrange the trip and indeed participating fully in the marriage—that Harry did not know how to ask for help. Further, I stressed that his inability to ask for and accept help had been at least partially responsible for the failure of his nursing home empire as well as his marriage. And it didn't seem to endear himself to his son either.

I stressed to Harry that it would be okay to ask for help, and that it would be healthy for him to drop his false sense of bravado. If he did so, he would be better able to make friends that he could trust. I pointed out to him that the attitudes toward life that his father expressed towards him when he was growing up had fixated him emotionally on not trusting anyone, and thus not being able to reach out.

Harry did not make any more suicide attempts in the time he was seeing me. He took my thoughts to heart and brought in a book that argued that if your business fails, it does not mean that you fail as a person. He even worked with me to make a film on forces leading to his crisis and began to practice medicine again in a limited fashion, despite losing his nursing home empire. Harry was beginning to learn how to take help. I have lost touch with Harry over the years, but I am hopeful that this process continued for him and he was able to build back a more limited life for himself. Imagine you are a psychotherapist or a clergy person.

If Harry came into your office, how would you describe him? What would be your diagnosis?

A. Grandiose

- B. Narcissistic: selfish and insensitive
- C. Full of himself, cocky
- D. Unable to trust others and accept help

Secondly, how would you treat him and help him realize he does not have to be a superman to be worthy?

- A. Help him learn to find *purpose* in the simple activities of day-to-day life.
- B. Help him accept his own limits and that he can't do everything himself.
- C. Develop a sense of humor.
- D. All of the above.

My Life Lesson

We end the discussion of Harry with an explication of the following life lesson. Harry had been searching for external events to give his life *meaning*. When his business failed largely due to his grandiosity, the entire false self he had created disintegrated. And he attempted to kill himself and failed. Only then did he begin to realize that he does not need to be driven to search for *meaning*. He had come to realize that his life has *purpose*. Just because his business had failed, it did not mean he had failed. He seems to have learned the lesson of Job. His life has intrinsic *purpose*. He does not need to go searching for it, and he did not try to commit suicide again in the time I was treating him. In fact, his entire mood had become more *purposive*.

7

The Importance of Hope

IN THE PREVIOUS CHAPTER, we discussed two clinical cases illustrating how the search for *meaning* can be detrimental, even suicidal. And these cases confirm the suicidal patterns among ancient Greek figures from the tragedies of Sophocles and Aeschylus, and even more so among the early Stoics, especially Zeno, the founder of the Greek Stoic school, and later Roman Stoics such as Cicero and both the older and younger Seneca. This proclivity is even reflected in the ancient Greek story of Pheidippides, which we have discussed in our introduction.

So now we must address a most serious question. What is *meaning* exactly, and why does the search for it so often lead to disastrous, even suicidal, outcomes? We have discussed at some length the strange suicidal death of Zeno the Stoic in this regard and that of Patient Charlotte. What *meaning* were they seeking and why did they not find *purpose* in their day-to-day lives? *Purpose* was inherent in the life of the biblical Job. He did not make his situation worse by catastrophizing even severe stressors in his life. Zeno the Stoic and Patient Charlotte took their lives over minor mishaps, while the biblical Job and patient Harry did not, despite suffering much worse calamities.

We would conjecture that Zeno the Stoic and Patient Charlotte committed suicide not because of the degree of external life stressors, but because each had a vulnerability. And what is this vulnerability? We would conjecture the vulnerability is the absence of an intrinsic sense of *purpose* in their lives, and moreover a *hopelessness* that derives from this absence, and a destructive search for *meaning*. In contrast, the biblical Job seems to possess an inherent sense of *hope* and thus a life *purpose*, while patient Harry seems to have developed it over the course of therapy. Why is this and what is the role of *hope* in ancient Greek and biblical thinking? As we can see, the presence or absence of *hope* is central in respective foundation stories of these respective cultures. And they could not be more different.

HOPE IS LOCKED UP IN GREEK NARRATIVES

Hesiod's account of the beautiful but amoral Pandora is sadly an account of how *hopeless* life is in ancient Greek thinking. It is not a stretch to say that Zeus, the head god in the Greek pantheon, had no real interest or compassion for man, and indeed may have feared being displaced by man if he empowered him. Prometheus ("forethought" in ancient Greek) and his half-brother, Epimetheus ("afterthought"), were cousins of Zeus who joined him in his war against his father, Cronus. They are assigned the responsibility of creating man. Prometheus shapes man out of mud and Athena, daughter of Zeus, breathes life into him. Prometheus had assigned Epimetheus the task of giving the creatures of the earth their various qualities, such as swiftness, cunning, strength, fur, and wings. Unfortunately, by the time he reaches man, Epimetheus has given out all the good qualities and there are none left for man.

The untrustworthy Zeus compounds the damage by deciding to make life difficult for men by withholding from them the knowledge of fire, presumably in retaliation for an experienced slight towards him on the part of Prometheus—Zeus had been offered a meat sacrifice without fat. Fire is critical to the generation of light and heat, necessary to hold the environment at bay and to provide the basis for technological and medical advance. By withholding this knowledge, Zeus, the father god, is keeping man subservient to nature. Prometheus rebels against Zeus (at least in part) in order to help man and does so, stealing fire from Mount Olympus, the home of the gods. Prometheus hides the fire in a hollow fennel stalk, and brings it to man, releasing him from his dependency. Zeus soon learns what has been done and, enraged, creates Pandora (meaning "all-gifted"), a beautiful but amoral and deceitful creature, as a punishment, and sends her to Epimetheus, the naïve half-brother of the wise Prometheus, along with a box as a "gift." One day, Pandora decides to open the box that Zeus has sent along with her. The box contains all the evils in the world, which fly out as soon as

Pandora opens it. She closes the lid as quickly as she can, but it is too late; only hope remains locked in the box, and unavailable to people.[1]

The Greek sense that hope is but an illusion is graphically illustrated in Sophocles' plays.

Oedipus himself says at the end of *Oedipus the King*:

> But now I am forsaken of the gods, son of a defiled mother, successor to his bed who gave me my own wretched being.[2]

And even more graphically at the end of Sophocles' *Antigone*:

> Pray thou no more, for mortals have no escape from destined woe.[3]

HOPE IS ACCESSIBLE IN BIBLICAL NARRATIVES

Biblical scriptures portray hope is a very different way. These qualities are central to the story of Noah and the flood. As the story begins, the biblical God sends the flood to destroy the men whom he had created because of their wickedness, corruption, and lawlessness. Yet God himself warns the just Noah of the coming flood and provides him with an exact blueprint for an ark that will save him and his family. After the flood, God places a rainbow in the heavens as a sign of his covenant with man that he will not send another flood to destroy man. The bow becomes the very symbol of hope.[4] We will discuss this story in greater detail in comparison to the parallel Greek flood story in chapter 8.

The sense of hope in the face of a seemingly hopeless situation is stated unconditionally in the Hebrew Bible.

> Cast me not out, neither forsake me, O God of my salvation, For though my father and mother have forsaken me, the Lord will take me up.[5]

And even more strongly in the Babylonian Talmud.

---

1. Hesiod, *Theogony*, ll. 533–615; *Works and Days*, ll. 53–105; Plato, *Protagoras* 320c–22a.
2. Sophocles, *Oedipus the King*, ll. 1359–61.
3. Sophocles, *Antigone* 1.1336.
4. Gen 6–9.
5. Ps 27:9–10.

THE IMPORTANCE OF HOPE 75

Even if a sword's edge lies on the neck of a man he should not hold himself back from prayer.[6]

GREEK FIGURES FACING INVOLUNTARY DEATH

In this context, let us compare the Greek and the biblical approaches to facing one's involuntary death. Let us first examine the Greek playwright Euripides' characters of Iphigenia, Macaria, and the conquered Trojan princess Polyxena as compared to that of Rabbi Akiba. Consider first the situation of Iphigenia. She accepts willingly, almost gladly, a seer's order that she must be sacrificed before her father's army will be able to sail for Troy. She grasps for a freedom that she does not have by trying to make her death seem voluntary instead of obligatory:

> I have chosen death: it is my own free choice. I have put cowardice away from me. Honor is mine now. O mother, say I am right.[7]

She sounds very much like Zeno the Stoic, in an attempt to exert control over a situation which she really does not have. This may well provide an illusory sense of *meaning* in her life, substituting for a genuine life purpose.

A second Greek character in Euripides facing certain death is Macaria, the daughter of Heracles. She appears in his play *The Trachinae*. After Heracles' death, his family seeks refuge in Athens from his old enemy, King Eurystheus of Argos, who wishes to kill them. Demophon of Athens is willing to help the fugitives, but an oracle pronounces that a girl of noble descent must be sacrificed to the goddess Persephone in order for him to defeat the Argives. Macaria takes the bait, revealing a willingness to let herself be sacrificed for others. She seems to find *meaning* in this action.

Death is welcome to her as long as it is glorious, and she has freely chosen it. A lottery is suggested involving Macaria and her sisters, but Macaria will have none of this. Her sacrifice for others has no *meaning* if it is imposed through a lottery, nor does she seem to want to avoid the sacrifice through winning the lottery:

> My death shall no chance lot decide, there is no graciousness in that peace ... But if ye accept and will avail you of my readiness, freely do I offer my life for those, and without constraint.[8]

6. BT, *Berachot*, 10a.
7. Sophocles, *Iphigenia in Aulis* 1375–77.
8. Sophocles, *Trachinae*, ll. 541–43.

Consider finally Euripides' *Hecuba*. Polyxena, prisoner of the Greek conquerors after the fall of Troy and the last surviving daughter of Queen Hecuba, is another altruistic suicide. Her sense of *noblesse oblige* makes it impossible for her to escape the ritual death demanded of her. The play commences with the Greek fleet ready to return home after sacking Troy. The ghost of Achilles appears and demands that a virgin be sacrificed on his tomb before the fleet can sail.

First, Polyxena expresses her sense of ruin and outrage: "For my own life, its ruin and its outrage, never a tear I shed; nay death is become to me a happier lot than life."[9] Like Iphigenia and Macaria, Polyxena seeks to create the illusion of control over her own death: "Of my free will I die; let none lay hand on me; for bravely will I yield my neck."[10] The Greeks are impressed with the bravery of their Trojan captive, and they unbind her. Polyxena then voluntarily tears open her robe, sinks to her knee, and bares her breast. Her need for *meaning* obliges leads her on to an altruistic suicide:

> Young prince, if 'tis my breast thou'dst strike, lo! Here it is, strike home! Or if at my neck thy sword thou'st aim, behold! That neck is bared."[11]

Each of these three characters behave like Zeno, trying to maintain an illusion of control to make their deaths appear voluntary in their desperate search for *meaning*. The hard reality is that they will be killed whether they agree to it or not. Turning their involuntary deaths into voluntary acts provides an illusion of control.[12]

BIBLICAL FIGURES FACING INVOLUNTARY DEATH

Contrast these Greek deaths with that of Rabbi Akiba in the early years of the second century CE, who was brutally tortured by the hands of the Romans for teaching Scripture. Akiba recited the Shema, the traditional Jewish prayer, "Hear O Israel, the Lord is our God, the Lord is one." By this, Akiba reconfirmed his faith in God and in life and did not need to

---

9. Euripides, *Hecuba*, ll. 210–11.
10. Euripides, *Hecuba*, ll. 559–62.
11. Euripides, *Hecuba*, ll. 563–65.

12. Perhaps this self-deception is what Frankl (*Man's Search for Meaning*, 83) is pinpointing in his insistence that in the world of Auschwitz, honesty demands the realization that hope is an illusion, yet people must hope against hope. "They must not lose hope but should keep their courage in the certainty that the hopelessness of the struggle did not detract from its dignity and its meaningfulness." But Frankl does not address the question of what forms the foundation of this hope.

seek illusory control by pretending to die willingly. He psychologically and spiritually was able to reject the idea of the Romans' control over his death, without resorting to a suicidal explanation—that he chose it willingly. His life had inherent *purpose* and he did not have to resort to artificial *meaning* interpretations when facing his death. He was not choosing to die, nor did he cede to the Romans' control over his death. It belonged to his God, the God of Scriptures.

Let us examine in this context the death of the late Joseph Cardinal Bernardin of Chicago, who presents a clear biblical contrast with regard to dealing with a great challenge in his life.[13] At sixty-eight, Bernardin received a diagnosis of terminal pancreatic cancer. He refused prolonged treatment, and said he found peace "by putting himself in God's hands." But he did not hasten his death or fight for a control of his death, as did our Patient Charlotte in the previous chapter.

Bernardin lived his life as fully as his strength allowed to the very end, completing many final tasks. Even more, Bernardin turned his dying process into one of his most profound teaching moments, living life with dignity and gracefulness till he was taken away. He did not need to catastrophize his situation, but indeed coped with the discomfort he must surely have been in and lived his life as purposively and fully as he could until the end. He finished a book on interfaith relations, saw friends and family for the last time, and wrote final letters and Chanukah and Christmas dards before he died. He did not try to milk his death for *meaning* missing in his life but accepted it as a natural part of the human condition. And he continued to live *purposively*.

We can never eliminate all suffering. Nor can those who see suffering as ennobling ask others, who may not share this view, to suffer as exemplars for the rest of us. Yet, we can hope to have some of the blessings that made it possible for Bernardin to die as he did. Bernardin's death also asks us to attend to how we live—to be open to giving and receiving love, and to understand that the choices we make affect not only our life but also our death. Thinking about the *meaning* of our lives is not a task for its last moment. The cardinal nurtured in us the courage to think about a good death for ourselves and those we love, and for holding out the hope that dying well is truly possible.

Note how different Bernardin's stance in this regard is from both Zeno the Stoic and Patient Charlotte. He did not catastrophize minor discomforts, but, like Job, accepted some pain and suffering. And furthermore, he did not focus on death, as did Zeno and the other Stoics, but rather on his whole life.

13. Holstein, "Dying Cardinal Bernardin's Way," 1.

THE SUNSET LIMITED

Consider the following situation. You are standing in a deserted subway station late at night, when somebody tries to jump to jump on the tracks in front of an oncoming train. What do you do? This is exactly the theme of a 2011 HBO movie directed by Tommy Lee Jones entitled *The Sunset Limited*.[14] This adaptation of Cormac McCarthy's play takes place in a single room and consists of only two men, neither of whom are ever named, throughout its ninety-minute running time. It takes place in New York City and stars Jones and Samuel L. Jackson. Jackson plays a black, intensely religious maintenance man who saves Jones's character, a disaffected, asocial white college professor, from suicide. Jones (offscreen) has tried to jump in front of a subway train, *The Sunset Limited*, as it roared through an otherwise empty subway station at Eighth Ave. and 155th St., and Jackson has prevented him from jumping.

Now the train is gone, and Jones's window for jumping in front of it has temporarily closed. He reluctantly goes to Jackson's apartment, where the two fall into an intense conversation about what just happened and why.

As the one (Jackson) attempts to connect on a spiritual and emotional (indeed, biblical) level, insisting his life has *purpose*, the other (Jones) remains steadfast in his Stoic despair and belief. His life has no *meaning*. Both passionately defend their personal credos and try to convert the other.

Jones says that at a certain point there's no alternative to suicide. He's tired of living; he's got nothing more to live for; whats the point? His life is *meaningless*. Jackson's character doesn't exactly try to answer that question. Instead, he argues that there is a *purpose* behind everything God does and our job here is to find it. Jackson's own humble life suggests belief is most of what he has. But that is enough, he says, to keep him going. It has helped him survive a stay in prison and keeps him getting by as a maintenance man living in a threadbare tenement apartment.

The dialogue in this movie is brilliant, but this is the problem. It is all dialogue. Jackson's character, to be sure, tries to puncture the self-contained and destructive logic of the brilliant Jones-played professor. He tries, but he tries verbally. There is very little hands-on intervention of the type employed in the biblical story of Elijah described earlier. There does not seem to be much, if any, food in the apartment (as the angel brought Elijah). Jackson's character attempts to give Jones' character coffee to drink, but offers him nothing to eat, nor does he suggest he lay down to rest. Nor is there little, if any, physical contact. Nor is there discussion of any other part of their lives.

---

14. Jones, *Sunset Limited*.

Jackson does not probe to find out what are the passions of Jones' life. He does not engage Jones as to what things give Jones' life *purpose*.

As the film ends, Jones insists on leaving Jackson's apartment. Jackson resists, trying to keep Jones safe in his apartment, but Jones insists Jackson unbolt his door. After Jackson opens the door, Jones leaves to what seems to be a very bleak fate. Jackson's entire intervention attempt has been undone by the fact that it largely remained on the verbal level that Jones could resist. This remains the Greek Stoic trap which keeps the saving biblical message of being loved by a concerned Creator at such a remote level that its life-affirming human warmth is not accessible.

ELIJAH AGAINST AJAX

Compare in this context the Greek story of Ajax and the biblical story of Elijah, both of which we have discussed briefly earlier in this book. Let us return to these narratives now.

The Suicide of Ajax

After the death of Achilles in the Trojan War, the Greek leaders choose Odysseus over Ajax to inherit his arms, making Ajax feel his honor is stained. Ajax sets out at night to murder Agamemnon, the leader of the Greek forces and Agamemnon's brother Menelaus. The goddess Athena becomes angry and makes Ajax insane. Ajax slaughters sheep in the army's flocks, and leads others to his tent, thinking that he is killing/torturing the Greek leaders themselves. As his madness passes, Ajax retreats humiliated and despondent into his tent, not disguising his suicidal thoughts.

Ajax cries, something he had always refused to do as it "befitted cowards only."[15] "Ah me, the mockery," he cries, and continues: "To what shame am I brought low."[16] Ajax is overwhelmed by what has happened to him and sees no way out other than suicide. He has not received positive support from others. A message to the Greek chieftains ordering that Ajax not leave his tent alone is sent too late by his half-brother, Teucer. Ajax has already fallen on his sword.[17]

---

15. Sophocles, *Ajax* 1.320.
16. Sophocles, *Ajax* l.365
17. Sophocles, *Ajax*, ll. 748–55, 848–49, 865.

The Suicide Prevention of Elijah

The prophet Elijah represents a contrasting example of how to treat a depressed and suicidal person. In the midst of an ongoing conflict with Jezebel, who wants to kill him,[18] Elijah is at the end of his rope, says he cannot go on, and expresses a wish to die.[19] God is portrayed as listening to his prophet Elijah and taking his statement to heart. Elijah lies down and sleeps under a broom tree, and an angel touches him and says to him:

> "arise and eat": and he looked, and behold, there was at his head a cake baked on the hot stones, and a cruse of water. And he did eat and drink and laid him down again. And the angel of the Lord came again the second time, and touched him, and said: "Arise and eat; because the journey is too great for thee." And he did eat and drink, and laid him down again and he arose, and did eat and drink, and went in the strength of that meal forty days and forty nights unto Horeb the mount of God.[20]

Elijah recovers his strength and goes to Mt. Horeb with the help of young Elisha.[21] These two narratives are contrasted in Table 5.

Table 5: Elijah against Ajax		
Stage	Ajax	Elijah
1. Precipitating stressor	Ajax is humiliated by both Agamemnon and Athena.	Elijah is overwhelmed and exhausted from his harassment by Queen Jezebel.
2. Reaction	Ajax says he wants to die.	Elijah says he wants to die.
3. Response of others	Ajax is allowed to leave his tent alone.	Elijah is sent an angel, who brings him food, drink, and companionship and lets him rest.
4. Effect	Ajax kills himself by falling on his sword.	Elijah recovers his strength and continues his mission in Horeb and is given help by the younger Elisha.

If the character played by Samuel Jackson in *The Sunset Limited* had only had tasty cakes and quenching drinks in his apartment, he might have been more successful in instilling a life *purpose* into the professor played by Tommy Lee Jones.

---

18. 1 Kgs 19:1–2.
19. 1 Kgs 19:3–4.
20. 1 Kgs 19: 5–8.
21. 1 Kgs 19:15–18.

8

Living Purposively versus Searching for Meaning

in Ten Areas of Life

IN THIS CHAPTER, WE will contrast ancient Greek versus biblical views with regard to ten areas of life. Each of these Greek views forces the human being to *search for meaning*. *Meaning* is assumed in the biblical views, allowing a person to *live purposively*. We will illustrate this difference in the following ten comparisons.

1. RELATING TO THE ENVIRONMENT

As discussed in chapter 1, the Greek and biblical creation stories embody two radically different worldviews. Nature precedes the gods in the Greek version, but God precedes nature in the biblical account. The differences in the respective orderings are not just chronological, but logical and psychological as well. Let us repeat what we wrote in chapter 1.

According to Hesiod, in the beginning there was *chaos*, which has often been interpreted as a moving formless mass, from which the cosmos and the gods originated.[1] The noun *xaos* refers to infinite space or time or

---

1. Hesiod, *Theogony* l.116.

the nether abyss, while the verb *xao* denotes "to destroy utterly."[2] *Chaos* has come to mean complete disorder and confusion. There is the implication *chaos* must be subdued and controlled for the world to be formed. Creation seems to be without *purpose* and the human being must search for *meaning*. This sounds quite similar to the emphasis of the Helter Skelter theme of the Manson gang.[3]

The biblical account of creation represents the exact opposite worldview. God precedes and indeed creates nature, nature representing the rules thaht God has put into place to create some order in the physical world he has created.

> In the beginning God created the heaven and the earth. Now the earth was unformed and void, and darkness was upon the face of the deep; and the spirit of God hovered over the face of the waters.[4]

God then proceeds to create form out of the unformed (*tohu vovohu*)—again, not by subduing *chaos* as in the Greek account. To emphasize, the biblical *unformed* is not equivalent to the Greek *chaos*. The biblical God is seen as a potter or a sculptor, not a jailor or a tyrant. Creation is inherently *purposive*.

The Greek Account

The Greek (and Roman) world seems to see the earth Gaia as a mother, a woman, and vacillates between idealizing her and raping her.

Evidence for the idealizing pole is provided by the environmental historian J. Donald Hughes, who argues that "the Greeks in particular thought that rearranging land and sea was a prideful challenge to Zeus, who had ratified their limits when he divided the world with his brothers."[5] Hughes offers the following example to support this thesis. When the people of Cnidus tried to dig a canal through the neck of land that connected them to Asia Minor, many injuries occurred to the workmen from flying rock splinters. They received the following explanation from the Oracle of Delphi: "Do not fence off the isthmus, do not dig. Zeus would have made an island had he willed it." They stopped work immediately.[6]

2. Liddell et al., *Greek-English Lexicon*.
3. Again see Bugliosi, *Helter Skelter*.
4. Gen 1:1–2.
5. Hughes, *Pan's Travail*, 51.
6. Herodotus, *Histories* 1.174.

Hughes provides another example to support his case regarding what was at times the ancient Greek unwillingness to alter the earth at all. During the invasion of Greece by the Persian king Xerxes, it was regarded as evidence of "pride going before a fall" that he had built a bridge of boats across the Hellespont, turning sea into land, and that he caused a canal to be cut though the Athos peninsula.[7]

On the other hand, the Greek attitude towards the earth sometimes seems to go to the opposite extreme, actually abusing if not raping her. While being somewhat unique in their fascination with science, the Greeks and later the Romans seemed to have been quite indifferent regarding certain ravages to their environment. Hughes points in particular to the problems of deforestation, overgrazing, and erosion. Plato, for example, observed that the heavily forested mountains of Attica had been laid bare by the cutting of timber and by grazing, resulting in an erosion of the rich and deep soil. As a consequence, the springs and streams had dried up.[8] Strabo offered a similar analysis, maintaining that the forests near Pisa had been exhausted by shipbuilding and the construction of buildings in Rome and villas in the surrounding countryside.[9]

The depletion of wildlife was also a problem and is reflected in the ambivalent Greek attitude towards the nature deity Artemis (adopted into the Roman pantheon as Diana). On the one hand, she was a protectress of wild animals; on the other, a hunter of them. According to a Greek myth, the mighty hunter Orion boasted that he would kill every wild beast in the world. In retaliation, Artemis, goddess of the wild, or in some versions Gaia, mother earth herself, retaliated by sending a giant scorpion to sting Orion. Zeus intervened and set both Orion and the scorpion in the sky as constellations opposite one another.[10] This clearly indicates a Greek awareness that wildlife might be destroyed. And there were attempts to protect animals within wildlife preserves. Sacrifices of wild animals as opposed to domestic animals were rare in Greek, though not in later Roman times, and wild animals in sanctuaries were preserved as sacred to the gods.[11] Nevertheless, the Greek fascination with hunting did tend to diminish certain animal species.

The situation seems to have become worse in later Roman times, though there were always important figures that stood up for animal rights.

7. Strabo, *Geographica*, 14, ll. 5.
8. Plato, *Critias* 11b-d.
9. Strabo, *Geographica*, 5, ll. 5.
10. Ovid, *Fasti* 5.539–41.
11. Birge, "Sacred Groves in the Ancient Greek Word"; Hughes, *Sacred Groves*.

Plutarch in particular exhibited respect, admiration, and sympathy for living creatures.[12] Nevertheless, Hughes argues that there is considerable doubt that this translated into practical programs to protect wildlife.[13] And even more devastatingly, the later Roman Empire was the scene of numerous circuses or *venationes* wherein thousands of wild animals were massacred for the entertainment of the public.[14]

All this can be seen as evidence of the basic lack of *purpose* in the Graeco-Roman world. Thus, stories emerge in an attempt to construct some kind of *meaning* in a person's life.

The Biblical Account

The biblical account of creation is very different. God exists prior to nature and in fact creates heaven and the earth. "In the beginning God created the heaven and the earth." God then proceeds to create order out of formlessness (*tohu vovohu*). First, lightness is divided from darkness. God then divides water from the land. At this point, God begins to prepare this world for the entrance of man. First he has the earth bring forth vegetation. He then places living creatures in the sea and fowls in the sky. Now God places living creatures on the earth, cattle, creeping things, and other beasts.[15]

The world is now ready for man in God's plan. There is no need to search for *meaning* as God creates in unconditional love the human being, male and female, his ultimate handiwork, in his own image and gives them dominion over all in nature he has created.[16] The upshot of this biblical account is that the human being is not driven by a *search for meaning*. Rather, the human being *has a purpose*: to help bring God's plan to fruition. Scriptures describe the world and all that is in it as created by God, in love for his creation.

Humankind is given dominion over all, and the first people are placed in the garden of Eden "to dress and keep it."[17] This is its *purpose*. It is incumbent on humanity not to wantonly destroy. Having dominion over the earth does not entitle man to misuse or abuse it. Nature is not presented as something alien to man; it is to be *neither* worshiped *nor* raped, but instead tended and cared for lovingly and carefully. The land of Israel was to

---

12. Plutarch, *Morals*, 999a.
13. Hughes, *Pan's Travails*, 111.
14. Friedlander, *Life and Manners*, 2:66.
15. Gen 1.
16. Gen 1:27–29.
17. Gen 2:15.

lie fallow one year out of every seven, and although the *purpose* was not specifically the replenishment of the soil, replenishment would serve as one benefit.[18]

"You shall not destroy" (*lo taschchlit*) is stated in the context of destroying trees but is understood in the rabbinic literature as including all sorts of wanton destruction.[19] All that God created has its own *purpose* and beauty. Midrash relates that David once did not understand why God needed to create spiders. Then a spider spun a web over the entrance to a cave where David was hiding so that his pursuers would not think of looking for him there.[20]

The medieval *Sefer Hachinuch* writes that the essence of this law is to teach people to love what is good and beneficial and to take care of it. "It is the way of pious people who love peace and rejoice in the good of the Creation that they would not destroy even a mustard seed and they will do all in their power to prevent needless destruction."[21]

In the same line of thinking, the Talmud says that one who destroys anything in anger is as though guilty of worshiping idols, in the sense that he obeys the destructive urges in his nature rather than connecting with God and the wonders of his creation.[22]

On the direct practical level, there are dozens of biblical laws that regulate in great detail what we may and may not do to the environment.[23] The Hebrew Scriptures prohibit the crossbreeding of different species of animals[24] as it bans the transplanting of branches of differing species of fruit trees[25] and the intermingling of seeds in planting.[26] Likewise, the Hebrew Bible prohibits various forms of activities that would involve cruelty to animals. We may not harness together animals of different strengths as it might create an unbearable load on the weaker.[27] We may not pass by an animal that has collapsed under its load, but are duty bound to help it.[28]

---

18. Lev 22:28.
19. Deut 20:19–20.
20. Alpha Beta Ben Sira 24a and b.
21. Sefer Hachinuch 529, 24b.
22. b. Shabbat 105b
23. Berman, Jewish Environmental Values, 199.
24. Lev 19:19.
25. Lev 19:19 as per Maimonides, Book of Commandments, Negative Commandment, No. 216.
26. Deut 22:9.
27. Deut 22:6–7.
28. Exod 23:5; Deut 22:4.

It is clear then that nature is not to be ravaged. However, nature is not to be worshiped in the Greek sense either. There are times when trees must be cut down in the service of human progress. This is the rabbinic understanding of the *Lo'Taschit* verse in Deuteronomy,[29] which literally bans *only* the destruction of *fruit-bearing* trees during war. Other trees may be destroyed and cut down in order to build bulwarks against the city that wars against one, until it is subdued.

Some Talmudic writings go even further in the furthering of human welfare even if it involves some destruction of the environment. Rabbi Berman points to the *Gemara* in *Baba Kamma*, which suggests that protection even of fruit-growing trees may be overridden by economic need.[30] Destruction for protection of health is permissible.[31] The *Gemara* in *Shabbat* goes even further in indicating that a psychological need or a personal aesthetic preference is sufficient to justify what would otherwise constitute a wasteful use of natural resources.[32]

Yet at the same time, all of God's creation, and even the incremental changes that humans have made to God's world, are entitled to be protected from wanton destruction. It is God and not humanity that is the continuing owner of all the earth.[33] In short, human needs must always be balanced against environmental concerns. It should be remembered that the biblical God does not attempt to withhold the knowledge of fire from man, as does Zeus. The implication of this is clear. Man is encouraged to incrementally improve on the environment as long as he does not wantonly destroy it. This implies an attitude of respectful stewardship rather than absolutist environmentalism or, worse, blind worship of nature. Environmental concerns must always be calibrated against human needs, and in the final analysis human needs will prevail. In the words of Rabbi Joseph B. Soloveitchik, a great contemporary interpreter of Jewish law, there is an unavoidable dynamic tension between the capacity to exercise control over nature and the duty to act toward nature with a sense of fiduciary responsibility.[34]

---

29. Deut 20:19–20.
30. b. Baba Kamma, 91b–92a
31. b. Shabbat, 128b–29a
32. b. Shabbat, 105b.140b.
33. Gen 1:26–28.
34. Soloveitchik, *Lonely Man*, 10–16.

2. EATING

Ancient Greeks and Romans have very different narratives regarding eating and meals than do the biblical and rabbinic Jews. While Greek and Roman narratives of meals often seem to encourage drunkenness (Greek) and gorging (Roman), biblical and rabbinic narratives of meals are *purposive* and encourage restraint.

Greek Narratives

According to the *Oxford Classical Dictionary*, meals were somewhat different in ancient Greece and Rome. Let us start with Greece, where people basically ate three meals daily: one a breakfast, which was taken right after sunrise; second, a main meal in the middle of the day; and, third, a dinner in the evening. For poorer people, the breakfast may have been substituted for lunch. Many of these meals seem to have been quite uneventful, though some may have been dedicated to a god and thus had a dimension of the sacred.[35] However, one gets the impression that for the wealthy the meal was but a prelude to the *symposium*, which occurred after the main meal.

The Greek *symposium*, traditionally translated as "banquet" or "gathering of drinkers," was only for men (except for musicians and courtesans) and divided into two parts. The first part involved eating with some wine consumed with foods such as toasted wheat, honey cakes, and various beans which were aimed at absorbing the alcohol drunk with the intention of prolonging the consumption of alcohol.[36]

There were some intellectual topics discussed at these symposia, and they even became a type of literary genre where conflicting speeches were given on a number of different topics of the day,[37] but they often degenerated at the end into drinking parties, music, dancing, and orgies of free sexual behavior. Participants often wore flowers, told riddles and fables, and played games.

Although many of the Greek symposia were dedicated to the "divine Home," Homer's *Odyssey*, in fact, presents a number of horrible *purposelessness* narratives of eating and drinking. Two separate narratives in Homer's *Odyssey* illustrate how alcohol and drugs can overcome a person's sense of *purpose*. The first involves the lotus-eaters, a tribe encountered by Odysseus

---

35. *Oxford Classical Dictionary*, 658.
36. Flacelière, *Daily Life in Greece at the Time of Pericles*, 212–13.
37. *Oxford Classical Dictionary*, 1028.

during his return from Troy.[38] The lotus-eaters lured Odysseus's scouts to eat an exotic plant of great sweetness. Eating this plant seemed to produce a mindless but happy forgetfulness. Eaters literally forgot everything—who they were, what they were doing, and where they were going—and had had to be physical pulled, even dragged, back to their rowing benches. They were actually chained to their benches to force them to row.

A second narrative in the *Odyssey* involving the temptress Circe shows how alcohol and drugs can make a person lose the sense of *purpose* that makes humans human.[39] Circe drugs the drink she gives to Odysseus's men and turns them into swine, making them forget about who they are and what they are doing.

Several other Greek narratives of eating highlight a trapped view of human existence. Consider Erysichthon, who wickedly chopped down an ancient huge oak tree that was sacred to Ceres, the goddess of grain. Ceres punished him by giving him an insatiable appetite. The more Erysichthon ate, the hungrier he became. He gorged all day at his parents' expense, yet grew hungrier and thinner the more he ate. His parents could no longer afford to feed him. Running out of money, Erysichton finally sold his own daughter for food. However, with Neptune's help, she changed her form and escaped her slavery. When Erysichthon learned that she had this ability, he continued to sell her into slavery over and over. Even this, however, did not supply him with enough food, and he finally devoured himself, limb by limb.[40] No resolution is provided for Erysichthon's tragic eating disorder other than his self-destruction.

Another Greek story of disordered eating involves Tantalus. Zeus. After being admitted to the Olympian banquets of nectar and ambrosia, Tantalus betrays Zeus's secrets and steals the divine food to share among his mortal friends. Later, when he is hosting a banquet for the Olympians, Tantalus realizes that he does not have enough food to feed the company, so he cuts up his own son, Pelops, and adds the pieces to the stew. The gods notice the human flesh in their stew and draw back in disgust. However, the goddess Demeter, still dazed by the abduction of her daughter Persephone, eats the flesh from the left shoulder of Pelops.

Tantalus is punished in Hades in two ways, placed standing in a lake adjacent to fruit trees with branches extending to his shoulders. A teetering rock hangs above him, threatening to fall. The water touches Tantalus's cheeks, but whenever he tries to take a drink, the water dries up. Whenever

---

38. Homer, *Odyssey*, 9, ll. 63–104.
39. Homer, *Odyssey*, 10, ll. 198—400.
40. Ovid, *Metamorphoses*, 8, ll. 705–864; Graves, *Greek Myths*, vol. 1, Ch 24, n4.

he wishes to of the fruit, the branches are blown by tufts of air up to the clouds. Tantalus is trapped in a vicious labyrinth, a riddle with no way out.[41]

Even worse are stories of actual cannibalism in the *Odyssey*. These stories reflect obstacles put in the way of Odysseus's *purposive* behavior in returning to Ithaca. Book 9 describes the one-eyed cyclops Polyphemus.

> So I (Odysseus) spoke, and out of his pitiless heart he answered me not a word, but sprang up, and laid his hands upon my fellows, and clutching two together as they had been whelps, to the earth, and the brain flowed forth upon the ground and the earth was wet. Then cut he them up piece-meal and made ready his supper. So he ate even as a mountain-bred lion, and ceased not, devouring entrails and flesh and bones with their marrow ... And after the Cyclops had filled his huge maw with human flesh, and the milk he drank thereafter there, he lay within the cave, stretched out among his sheep.[42]

Book 10 of the *Odyssey* tells an equally disgusting story. Odysseus and his companions land in their twelve ships at the mountain stronghold of Lamus, Telepylos of the Laestrogons. The Lastrogons are giant cannibals. Their king, Antiphates, eats on sight a scout Odysseus has dispatched to gain information as to the inhabitants of the island. As it were, eleven of Odysseus's ships have moored in the harbor, but Odysseus's own ship is moored outside the harbor. Antiphates leads the other giant cannibals to join him in smashing the moored ships in order to eat the men on board. They shoot spears at the men and bring them to a feast where they are the meal. Odysseus's ship alone gets away and he escapes.[43]

Although the Greeks viewed cannibalism (*anthropophagy*) as occurring among non-Hellenic barbarians, or else relegated to a world existing before the coming of the Olympian gods, the ubiquitousness of these stories in Greek mythology, in particular cannibalism of close family members, makes one pause and wonder. Why was their such fascination among the Greeks with these disgusting stories, all of which emphasize the lack of *purpose* in family life? For example, the vicious and disgusting narratives of Pentheus

---

41. Graves, *Greek Myths*, Vol. 2 Ch. 108; Apollodorus, *Library*, Epitome 2.1; Shoham, *Myth of Tantalus*.
42. Homer, *Odyssey*, 9, ll. 290–306.
43. Homer, *Odyssey*, 10, ll.56–102.

and the maenads,[44] Tereus and Procne,[45] and Thyestes and his son[46] all emphasize a profound lack of *purpose* in family life, at the very least.[47]

44. Euripides in the *Bacchae* and Ovid in the *Metamorphoses* portray King Pentheus's attempt to stop the Maenads, mad women raging upon the mountains in a destructive search for *meaning*, from tearing apart live animals limb from limb (*sparagmos*) and eating them raw (*omophagia*). However, inflamed by wine and religious ecstasy, the Maenads see Pentheus and tear off one arm after another. His mother, Agave, sees the wounded man, who calls out to her for help. Not recognizing he is her son, Agave tears off his head, celebrating her achievement, and brings it on a plate of her father, Cadmus, thinking it is that of a lion. Cadmus of course realizes that the head is that of his grandson and Agave's son, Pentheus. As Agave descends from her ecstatic madness, she realizes to her horror what she had done (Euripides, *Bacchae*, in Oates and O'Neill, *Complete Greek Drama*, 22:227–89; Ovid, *Metamorphoses* 3.655–733; Graves, *Greek Myths*, 1:27f.).

45. Tereus was a Thracian king and the husband of Procne. They had a son, Itys. Tereus lusted after his wife's sister, Philomela. Tereus raped her, and then to keep her from telling anyone, Tereus cut out Philomela's tongue and imprisoned her so she could never reveal what happened. If this wasn't bad enough, he then lied to his wife, Procne, telling her that her sister had died. But Philomela outsmarted him, weaving letters in a tapestry exposing and describing Tereus's crime. She was able to send this tapestry secretly to Procne. In revenge, Procne joined with Philomela in murdering her and Tereus's son, Itys, and serving his flesh in a meal to Tereus. Upon learning of Procne's and Philomela's ghastly deed, he tried to kill the two sisters but both were changed by the Olympian gods into birds (Ovid, *Metamorphoses* 6.426–710).

46. When Atreus discovered that Thyestes had committed adultery with his wife, Aerope, he became understandably enraged. To compound the damage, Thyestes killed one of Atreus's sons to save his own. Atreus pretended to forgive Theseus and sent a messenger to him with an offer to share of kingdom if he would return to Mycenae. However, as soon as Thyestes accepted his offer, Atreus killed Thyestes' three sons on the very altar of Zeus on which they had sought refuge. Atreus also killed Thyestes' infant twin sons. Upon Thyestes' return, Atreus welcomed him in the most gruesome manner. He cut up their bodies and served Thyestes pieces of their flesh, boiled in a caldron. After Thyestes had finished eating his meal, Atreus sent in another dish, containing the bloody heads and feet and hands of the infants, to bring home to Atreus what he had done. Thyestes fell back vomiting and laid a curse upon the house of Atreus (Hyginus, *Fabulae*, 88, 246, 258; Graves, *Greek Myths*, 2:111g.).

47. Portions of the narratives regarding both of Tereus and Procne, and also of Atreus and Thyestes, reappear In Shakespeare's *Titus Andronicus*. The eponymous Titus, a Roman general, returns from five years of war with the captured Tamora, queen of the Goths, and, in accordance with Roman rituals, sacrifices her eldest son to his own dead sons. This of course provokes Tamora's hatred and desire for revenge, which she accomplishes in spades. She and her love, Aaron the Moor, and their men capture one of Titus's surviving sons and tell Titus and his son that they will return the son unharmed if Titus will cut off his own arm and send it to them. Titus does and they return the son's head to Titus. Her revenge unsatisfied, Tamora urges her two remaining sons to rape Titus's daughter, which they do. Then, echoing Tereus's actions toward Philomena, they cut off her tongue and hands so she cannot accuse them publicly. Titus's revenge is similar to that of Atreus to Thyestes. He kills Tamora's sons, makes pie out of them, and feeds this pie to Tamora in the final scene of the play. Shakespeare's Roman Titus is no less barbaric than the barbarian.

A Roman Narrative

No eating narrative exemplifies a jaded lack of *purpose* and of any coherent order more than Petronius's description in *Satyricon* of the banquet of Trimalchio, a wealthy but jaded Roman.[48] While he was writing satire, Petronius, a freedman, seems quite miserable. He depicts wealthy Romans living in a disillusioned and vicious manner. Trimalchio himself is ostentatious to the extreme. After getting acclimated in the halls and baths,[49] the guests (mostly freedmen) come into the dining room per se. Petronius describes frescoes from "scenes from the *Iliad* and the *Odyssey*" and "gladiator games given by Laenas."[50]

Trimalchio seems to be trying to put on a big show to impress his guests. To directly quote Petronius:

> On a large tray stood a donkey made of rare Corinthian bronze; on the donkey's back were two panniers, one holding green olives, the other, black. Flanking the donkey were two side dishes, both engraved with Trimalchio's name and the weight of the silver, while in dishes shaped to resemble little bridges there were dormice, all dipped in honey and rolled in poppy seed ... Trimalchio was carried in, propped up on piles of miniature pillows in such a comic way that some of us couldn't resist impolitely smiling.[51]

Trimalchio is incontinent and makes many trips to the toilet. This allows the guests the space to talk to each other more openly.[52] The guests seem not to have any serious conversations, but are just making small talk, reflecting the emptiness of the upper-class Roman society.

Upon Trimalchio's return, the meal resumes.[53] There is a play within a play, which is aimed at tricking the diners. Nothing is what it seems; servants are humiliated for the amusement of the diners, and the emotions of the diners themselves are played with. Let us read Petronius's exact words: "Trimalchio had been scrutinizing the pig very closely and suddenly roared, 'What! What's this? By god, this hog hasn't even been gutted! Get that cook in here on the double ... Strip that man.'"[54] Taking Trimalchio seriously, the

---

48. Petronius, *Satyricon, v. Dinner with Trimalchio*.
49. Petronius, *Satyricon, v. Dinner with Trimalchio* 27.
50. Petronius, *Satyricon, v. Dinner with Trimalchio* 29.
51. Petronius, *Satyricon, v. Dinner with Trimalchio* 31.
52. Petronius, *Satyricon, v. Dinner with Trimalchio* 41.
53. Petronius, *Satyricon, v. Dinner with Trimalchio* 47.
54. Petronius, *Satyricon, v. Dinner with Trimalchio* 49.

guests plead that the man not be whipped. Trimalchio then grins at his joke and returns to the cook his clothes which had been taken from him. Now, Trimalchio orders the cook to gut the pig in front of the guests. The cook cuts the stomach of the pig, and out pours "not the pig's bowels and guts, but link upon link of tumbling sausages and blood puddings."[55] The chef is then presented with a silver crown and is honored by being offered a drink served on a Corinthian bronze platter.[56] As if this could undo his previous humiliation.

Supernatural stories about a werewolf and witches are then told.[57] Following a lull in the conversation, Scintilla, the wife of stonemason Habinnas, gets into a conversation with Trimalchio's wife, Fortunata, with regard to their jewelry.[58] Then Trimalchio sets forth his will and gives Habinnas instructions on how to build his monument when he is dead.[59]

Encolpius and his companions, by now tired, weary, and disgusted with all this ostentatious prattle, try to leave as the other guests proceed to the baths. However, they are prevented by a porter.[60] When Trimalchio holds a mock funeral for himself, Encolpius and his companions attempt to escape what has become a terribly oppressive experience. However, they are stopped by a porter and remain trapped. However, fortuitously, a horn sounds and the watchman misinterpret this as warning that a fire has broken out and burst into the residence. Encolpius and his companions takes advantage of this confusion and with his companions flees as if from a real fire.[61]

It would be difficult to conjure up a more frenetic, chaotic, and *purposeless* experience than Trimalchio's dinner. It truly represents searching for *meaning* in all the wrong places.

Biblical Narratives

What seems to be missing in Greek and Roman narratives of food and drink is an underlying sense of intrinsic *purpose*. The Hebrew Scriptures develop the approach that eating and drinking, like all activities of this earth, should be sanctified and made into a form of service to God. In this regard, biblical and postbiblical society celebrated many festivals, including the harvest,

---

55. Petronius, *Satyricon, v. Dinner with Trimalchio* 49.
56. Petronius, *Satyricon, v. Dinner with Trimalchio* 50.
57. Petronius, *Satyricon, v. Dinner with Trimalchio* 63–64.
58. Petronius, *Satyricon, v. Dinner with Trimalchio* 66.
59. Petronius, *Satyricon, v. Dinner with Trimalchio* 71.
60. Petronius, *Satyricon, v. Dinner with Trimalchio* 72.
61. Petronius, *Satyricon, v. Dinner with Trimalchio* 78.

weddings, the Sabbath, and of course the Passover Seder, which will be discussed in more detail below. A critical aspect of a biblical view of eating is mindful attention paid to the food that one eats. The meal is seen as an ordered activity, with each food blessed as an acknowledgment of the Creator's purpose in providing food for the human being. Whether one is formally religious or not, this has the effect of focusing one's attention on what one is eating. Unlike the often frightening and disgusting narratives in Greek mythology regarding food, some of which we have discussed previously, biblical narratives emphasize a positive *purpose*.

One of the earliest commandments in the Hebrew Bible, for example, is the prohibition against eating the sciatic nerve, specifically of kosher animals. This practice comes from the story of Jacob wrestling with the angel. Jacob returned to Canaan with his household after many years of sojourning with his tricky father-in-law, Laban, in Haran. He helped his family to cross the River Jabok, a tributary of the Jordan, and then went back across alone to bring a few remaining items.

> And someone wrestled with him until the morning star rose.
> And he (the angel) saw he could not overcome him (Jacob), so
> he touched the sinew of his thigh and dislocated the sinew of
> Jacob's thigh as he wrestled with him.[62]

The angel then told Jacob to let him go, but Jacob would not release the angel until he would bless Jacob. The angel then blessed Jacob, saying that he would no longer be called Jacob, denoting one who tried to grab his brother Esau, as well as others, by the heel (stealthily). Instead his name would be called Israel, designating one who had struggled with both God and men and had prevailed. The angel did indeed bless Jacob, recognizing Jacob's greatness and his growth. The sun now rose, and the angel had gone, and Jacob limped on his sore leg toward the frightening uncertainty of his meeting with Esau his brother, who had once sworn to kill him. The account goes on to relate that "the Children of Israel will not eat the sciatic nerve to this day because he (the angel) had touched the sinew of Jacob's thigh on the sciatic nerve."[63]

Other *purposive* guides to eating are a prohibition against slaughtering a mother and its young on the same day,[64] as we may not take the fledglings

---

62. Gen 32:23–33.
63. These passages have been originally translated by Matthew B. Schwartz.
64. Lev 22:28.

while the mother bird hovers over them.⁶⁵ On three occasions, Scripture warns against cooking the kid in its mother's milk.⁶⁶

Genesis 9:4 specifically forbids eating the flesh of living creatures (*ever min ha'hai*). Furthermore, Leviticus 17 is clear in its prohibition of eating the blood of living creatures:

> And whatsoever man there be of the hope of Israel, or of the strangers that sojourn among them, that eateth any manner of blood. I will set My face against that soul that eateth any manner of blood, I will set My face against that soul that eateth any manner of blood. and I will cut him off from among his people. For the life of the flesh is in the blood; and I have given it to you upon the altar to make atonement for your souls; for it is the blood that maketh atonement for your souls; for it is the blood that maketh atonement by the reason of life. Therefor I said unto the children of Israel: No soul of you shall eat blood, neither shall any stranger that sojourneth among you eat blood.⁶⁷

This view is enhanced by the Midrashic account of God's teaching Adam to make fire from rubbing flints together—we have discussed this in the previous section.⁶⁸ This, of course, allows people to cook meat, draining the blood from it, and is in total opposition to the aforementioned Greek account of Zeus's trying to withhold the knowledge of fire from man.⁶⁹

The Bible presents many laws and ideas regarding what kinds of animals, fish, and birds may or may not be eaten. But there is an area of thinking that goes beyond the stated rules and their interpretations. The book of Leviticus clearly instructs us: "Do not do anything disgusting."⁷⁰ One of the most striking illustrations of this is the biblical prohibition, given three separate times, against boiling a kid (a young goat) in the milk of its mother.⁷¹

Anything "disgusting," whether in food or behavior, brings one to transgress the aforementioned law of "Do not do anything disgusting." The commentaries provide multiple examples. One who drank from a vessel used previously to collect blood has violated this law. One must not drink from a glass left uncovered for a long time in regions where snakes or scorpions or

---

65. Deut 22:6.
66. Deut 14:21; Exod 23:19; 24:26.
67. Lev 17:10–14.
68. Gen. Rab. 11:2.
69. Hesiod, *Theogony* 556–613.
70. Lev 11:11.
71. Exod 23:19; 34:26; Deut 14:21.

other dangerous beasts might touch it. A person should not drink anything that disgusts him, including water from a chamber pot and certainly not vomit. Nor should one eat with soiled hands or from a dirty dish.

What is the *purpose* of the Hebrew Scripture permitting certain animals for food while forbidding others? Scholars offer a variety of explanations. Maimonides maintains that the forbidden foods are unhealthy or dirty. The Torah generally enjoins clean habits of living—all the more so regarding food. Pigs, he writes, live in filth and openly so in Western European towns.[72]

Despite presenting many laws and ideas regarding eating and foods, the Hebrew Bible surprisingly does not state a direct prohibition against cannibalism per se. However, Leviticus 11:2 says, "These are the living things which you may eat among all the beasts on the earth," followed by an enumeration of the permitted foods. Since no mention is made of human flesh, Maimonides argues that a prohibition against cannibalism may be inferred.[73]

Further, the Bible ordains that some foods may be eaten while others are prohibited, and people must express gratitude to God for their food.[74] Eating is *purposive* and a form of expressing and contributing to the joy of life and of marking special occasions such as the festivals mentioned above. Both the nutrition and the pleasure of eating offer people a means of enjoying and sanctifying God's creation and their role in it.

Let us conclude this section with a brief description of the Passover seder, which provides as striking a contrast with the previously discussed banquet of Trimalchio, as one might imagine.

There are fourteen steps in the Seder, described in the Passover Haggadah. The list of the steps is usually sung at the beginning of the Seder. We follow the steps one by one in the Haggadah.[75]

---

72. Maimonides, *Guide to the Perplexed* 3.48.

73. Maimonides, *Mishnah Torah, Ma'akhalot Asurot* 2:3. To be sure, cannibalism is mentioned several times in the Hebrew Bible (Lev 26:29; Deut 28:53–57; Jer 19:9; Lam 2:20; 4:10; Ezek 5:10). However, the practice is not condoned and is regarded as a product of almost inhuman desperation, whose occurrence is seen as a consequence of disobedience to God's laws (Lev 26:29, Deut 28:53–57; Jer 19:9; Lam 2:20; 4:10; Ezek 5:10). People were being starved to death during the siege of Samaria and would cannibalize their own children as the prophets predicted would happen if the Israelites forsook God (2 Kgs 6:28–29). This physical degradation was seen as accompanying the degradation of spiritual decay and apostasy.

74. Deut 8:10.

75. Goldberg, *Passover Haggadah*, , Toby Lausin (https://www.haggadoth.com/contributors-details/tobylausin).

1. *Kadesh*: Recitation of the kiddush (blessing over the first glass of wine).
2. *Urchatz*: Washing one's hands to be ritually clean in preparation for the next step of Seder.
3. *Karpas*: Eating the vegetable dipped into vinegar or saltwater, which is distributed to everyone at the table. Saltwater is symbolic of the tears shed by the Israelites in Egypt during slavery.
4. *Yahatz*: Breaking the middle matza and hiding half for Afikoman ("dessert"). The smaller piece is returned to the Pesach plate to be eaten later for the mitzvah of matzah. The larger piece, representing the Pesach sacrifice, is to be eaten at the end of the meal.
5. *Maggid*: Telling the story of Passover. The youngest child asks the four questions. The second cup of wine is drunk. The four questions are as follows: a) On all other nights we eat either leavened bread or unleavened bread (matzah); on this night why do we eat only unleavened bread? b) On all other nights we eat herbs of any kind; on this night why only bitter herbs? c) On all other nights we do not dip our herbs even once; on this night why do we dip them twice? d) On all other nights we eat our meals in any manner; on this night why do we sit around the table together in a reclining position? The matzah is uncovered and the story of the Israelites' exodus from Egypt is told as an answer to the four questions.
6. *Rachtzah*: Washing hands before meal, as is done before every meal. The second cut of wine is drunk.
7. *Motzi and Matzoh*: Say the blessing over the matza and eat it.
8. *Maror*: Eating the bitter herb, which is dipped into charoset (a mix of nuts, apples, cinnamon and wine).
9. *Korech*: Eating bitter herb and matza together as a sandwich
10. *Shulchan Orech*: Eating the festive meal. The term "Shulchan Orech" actually means "set table" or "ordered table."
11. *Tsafon*: Eating the *Afikoman*, which symbolizes the Pesach sacrifice, which in ancient times was eaten at the end of the meal.
12. *Barech*: Saying a blessing after the meal. The third cup of wine is drunk. The cup of Elijah the prophet is filled.
13. *Hallel*: Reciting a selection of chapters of Psalms.
14. *Nirtzah*: Singing of hymns that conclude the Seder. The fourth cup of wine is drunk. An additional prayer recites the hope that the next Seder will be conducted in Jerusalem.

According to Exodus, the biblical God instructs Moses and Aaron regarding the practices of the paschal service in Egypt. This was a decisive historical moment which should be actively and accurately remembered forever in its many details and implanted in the national consciousness. The Israelites began the process as slaves and completed the exodus as free people.

What can be more *purposive* than this?

3. RELATING TO ILLNESS

Throughout their history, the Jewish people have been greatly involved in medical science. At the same time, biblical ideas did not seem to influence Jewish physicians, who were completely under the influence of the Roman physician Galen. As Suessman Muntner notes,

> It is surprising to note that Talmudic pathology seems to have had no impact on medieval medicine, not even on the great Jewish physicians of the Middle Ages, such as Moses Maimonides and Isaac ben Solomon Israeli (I. Judaeus), who were thoroughly familiar with the Talmud. Medieval medicine was so completely under the spell of [the Roman physician] Galen that anything he ever said about medicine was accepted as infallible, while the health rules of the Talmud were ignored . . . *The Talmud was regarded as a purely religious code and not as a medical treatise of any kind.*[76]

It was not until 1911 that Jacob (Julius) Preuss published a systematic biblical view of anatomy, epidemiology, surgery, dentistry, otology, neurological disorders, obstetrics, and mental disease.[77] Nevertheless, a Hebrew basis for medicine is far from achieving widespread acceptance or even acknowledgment.[78]

Perhaps the single most important distinction between a Greek and biblical approach to medicine lies in their different approaches to treating a disease versus a whole person. This difference is dramatically illustrated in the contrast between the so-called Hippocratic oath and the physician's prayer attributed, perhaps incorrectly, to Maimonides.

---

76. Muntner, "Medicine in Ancient Israel," in Rosner, *Medicine in the Bible and the Talmud*, 20. Emphasis mine.

77. Preuss, *Biblical and Talmudic Medicine*.

78. See Schwartz and Kaplan, *Biblical Stories for Psychotherapy and Counseling*; Kaplan et al., "Biblical View of Health, Sickness and Healing"; Kaplan and Cantz, *Biblical Psychotherapy*.

The Greek Approach: The Hippocratic Oath

Hippocrates' view can be summarized as follows: 1) The physician is the servant of the "art" or "nature." 2) The "art" consists of three parties: the disease, the patient, and the physician. 3) The disease is the enemy, something to be combated by the patient along with the physician. 4) With regard to the disease, the physician is exhorted to do good or to do no harm. 5) In the Hippocratic oath, the physician swears to "give no deadly medicine to anyone, if asked, nor suggest any such counsel."[79]

The Jewish Approach: The Prayer of Maimonides

The physician's prayer attributed to Maimonides is fundamentally different: 1) The physician has been chosen by God to watch over the life and health of his creatures. 2) The physician prays for inspiration from God for love for his art and for God's creatures. There are three involved parties: God, the physician, and God's creature (the patient). 3) The disease is a beneficent messenger sent by God to foretell approaching danger and to urge the patient to avert it. 4) The physician has been chosen by God in his mercy to watch over the life and death of his creatures. 5) The physician specifically prays to remove from his patients "all charlatans and the whole host of officious relatives and know-all nurses, cruel people who arrogantly frustrate the wisest purposes of our art and often lead Thy creatures to their death."[80]

A Comparison

The most important distinction between Hippocrates and Maimonides may be in their contrasting views of disease. In the Hippocratic oath, the disease is the enemy, and the fight of the physician is to eradicate the disease or to cure the symptom. The patient seems secondary to this—a battlefield rather than a living person. This approach seems more like a power struggle between the physician and the disease—in an attempt to achieve some sort of *meaning* for the physician. It does not seem to be addressed toward the patient per se.[81]

---

79. Edelstein, *Hippocratic Oath*.

80. Golden, *Maimonides' Prayer for Physicians*.

81. The author remembers quite well his late mother complaining when she was treated for lymphoma: "They may be killing the disease, but they are killing me with it." Thankfully she survived, though one might look at some of Patient Charlotte's complaints regarding her hospital stay in chapter 6 in a different light.

In the prayer attributed to Maimonides, in contrast, the physician must treat the person (God's creature) and the disease as a symptom, an ally warning the physician of danger to the patient and as a signal to avert it. This view could not be more purposive and resonates quite well with more modern views of disease, especially with regard to disorders of the immune system.

4. OBEDIENCE VERSUS DISOBEDIENCE TO AN AUTHORITY

Let us consider now a fourth area of life where searching for *meaning* can be differentiated from living *purposively*. This is the question of obedience versus disobedience to an authority, one of the most vexing questions in society. One of the most widely cited series of experiments in modern social psychology is Stanley Milgram's study of obedience.[82] In this basic study, over half of the "teachers" (in reality, the subjects of the experiment) continue to apply "dangerous severe shocks to the "learner-confederate," who has stated that he has a heart condition, and stopped answering at a certain point.

This study was designed to model the behavior of Nazi war criminals and to belittle the defense used at Nuremberg that they were "just following orders." However, this message may have been overlearned and thus mislearned. The mantra of the West has come to be a distrust of authority per se (i.e., parents, community and religious leaders, and law and system of morality) rather than of a particular authority. This has led to an endless search for *meaning* in rebellion. But can following orders or instructions from an authority sometimes be *purposive*?

Albert Camus writes that revolt, revolution, and striving for freedom are inevitable aspects of human existence but warns us that we must observe limits to avoid having these admirable pursuits end in tyranny.[83] Let us compare Greek and biblical narratives with regard to accepting or questioning authority with regard to two major life events: first, the human acquisition of fire, and second, the human response the great flood.

---

82. Milgram, *Obedience to Authority*.
83. Camus, *Rebel*.

The Greek Account of Man's Acquisition of Fire

Zeus, the father of the gods in the Greek pantheon, has no real interest in man, nor compassion for him. As mentioned previously, Prometheus and Epimetheus are assigned the responsibility of creating man. Epimetheus has given all the good qualities out and there are none left for man. But Zeus is untrustworthy and compounds the damage by deciding to make life difficult for the first men by withholding from them the knowledge of fire. Fire is critical to the generation of light and heat to hold the environment at bay to provide the basis for technological advance. By withholding this knowledge, Zeus, the father god, is keeping man subservient to nature. Prometheus, the son god, rebels against Zeus to empower the man whom he (Prometheus) has created. Let us reemphasize the fact that Prometheus must steal fire for man from Mount Olympus, the home of the god. He hides it in a hollow fennel stalk and brings it to man, enabling him to survive. As man sees the gods are stacked against him, he cannot trust them and must continue to look for clues in his environment to survive. He is continuously looking for the *meaning* of events, sometimes physical and sometimes more spiritual, to make sense of the hostile environment into which he has been thrust.

The Biblical Account of Man's Acquisition of Fire

The biblical account is diametrically different. God himself creates man in his own image as his ultimate handiwork and gives him dominion over the world. He does not want man to be subservient to nature. Rather than withholding fire from man to keep him dependent, Jewish midrash portrays God as providing the means for Adam to invent fire because he has compassion for him.[84] Therefore, man does not need to rebel against God to gain autonomy. By trusting God, his life is *purposeful*.

The Greek Account of the Great Flood

A similar contrast emerges in a comparison of the Greek and biblical stories of a great flood, which probably occurred throughout the Fertile Crescent with the melting of the Ice Age. Let us begin with the Greek account.

Zeus, out of personal pique, sends a great flood to destroy mankind. Deucalion and Pyrrha survive by building a boat on the sly with help from their benefactor Prometheus, who provides a blueprint without Zeus's

---

84. m. Gen. Rab. 11:2.

knowledge. When the flood is over, Deucalion sacrifices to Zeus, who allows him to rebuild the human race. Zeus has the last laugh, however, for mankind is created from stones cast separately by Deucalion and Pyrrha over their shoulders. Deucalion's stones become men and Pyrrha's become women.[85]

Several points stand out in this narrative. First, Zeus orders the flood out of a sense of personal affront rather than any sort of moral reason. Second, once again, Prometheus must rebel against Zeus to preserve mankind. Thirdly, men and women are perceived as emerging from separate sources, rather than from joint parentage. Deucalion clones men, and Pyrrha women. This feeds into idea of the basic incompatibility between men and women and the idea that men are from Mars and women from Venus, to employ a modern metaphor.[86] Finally, there is no guarantee that Zeus will not send another flood if he so chooses. In short, human beings cannot trust Zeus and must continuously *search for meaning* dealing with an untrustworthy authority figure.

The Biblical Account of the Great Flood

The biblical narrative of the great flood is very different.[87] First, God sends the flood to destroy the men whom he had created because of their wickedness, corruption, and lawlessness, not out of any personal affront. Second, God saves Noah and his wife because they have obeyed his laws.[88] Noah is described as a just man and perfect in his generation and as "walking with God." Noah does not need to rebel against God, like Prometheus. Rather, God himself warns Noah of the coming flood and provides him with an exact blueprint for an ark which will save him. Thirdly, God has instructed Noah to bring male and female of each species on board the ark. After the flood ceases, all the living creatures, male and female, come out from the ark and repopulate the earth through their sexual union, the very antithesis of each gender cloning its own. Finally, God places a rainbow in the heavens

---

85 Apollodorus, *Library* 1.7.2.

86. Gray, *Men Are from Mars, Women Are from Venus*.

87. Gen 6–9.

88. In both the creation and flood narratives, the Greek account postulates a split between the destructive and vengeful father and the savior son who intervenes for mankind. The account in the Tanakh, in contrast, portrays the single God being intimately concerned with the welfare of the people he has created. The Christian contrast of the vengeful, capricious father god (Yahweh) of the "Old Testament" with the merciful son god (Jesus) of the "New Testament" reflects an unfortunate Greek read of the Hebrew Scriptures.

as a sign of his covenant with man that he will not send another flood to destroy man. We have discussed this earlier in this book as a sign of hope itself. This assurance allows the human being to *live purposively* rather than be constantly *searching of an illusory meaning* or clue that the world might end.

5. MEN AND WOMEN

The difference between the Greek and biblical accounts of the relationship between man and woman also can be seen through this lens of contrasting *searching for meaning* with *living purposively*. The Greek Pandora is described as a curse to man in retaliation for Prometheus stealing fire for man. The biblical Eve, in contrast, is described as a blessing to man and as a "helpmeet opposite" (*ezer kenegdo*).

The Greek Account

In the Greek account, Prometheus steals fire from Mount Olympus, the home of the gods, and, hiding it in a hollow fennel stalk, brings it to man, enabling him to survive.[89] Zeus soon learns what had been done and, enraged, creates Pandora, a beautiful but deceitful creature, as a punishment, and sends her along with a box as a "gift" to Epimetheus, the naïve half-brother of the wise Prometheus. One day, Pandora decided to open the box that Zeus had sent along with her. The box contains all the evils in the world, which fly out as soon as Pandora opens it. She closes the lid as quickly as she can, but it is too late; only hope remains locked in the box, and unavailable to people.[90]

Given this account, how can man trust woman? He is always on the alert that she will use her wiles to bring about his ruin. He is inherently suspicious, looking for *meaning* in all her actions. Is she *for* him, or *against* him? In this Greek account, fire gives man some autonomy, but the beautiful Pandora ruins everything. Woman does not simply domesticate man but brings about his ruin, stripping him of any autonomy he may achieve. Woman is seen as the castrator of man and a sexual relationship as a not-so-tender trap and man's undoing.[91] Consider *hystera*, the Greek term for the womb, from which English words like "hysteria" and "hysterectomy" emerge in our psychiatric and medical vocabulary. The *hystera* is a source of labile

---

89. Hesiod, *Works and Days*, ll. 50–157; *Theogony*, ll. 565–671.
90. Hesiod, *Works and Days*, ll. 47–104; *Theogony*, ll. 557–602.
91. Apollodorus, *Library* 1.

and even mercurial affect. No wonder Greek man fears female sexuality! Yet avoiding marriage leaves man alone in his old age.[92] So ancient Greek man is inherently ambivalent about woman, always on guard, and continuously *searching for meaning*

The Biblical Account

The creation of people in Genesis is different. It is the culmination of six days of creation by a benevolent and all-wise God. With all Adam's achievement, he is very alone. God sees that it is not good for a man to be alone, so, according to the second creation story in Genesis, he puts Adam into a deep sleep and separates part of his body, thus dividing the original human into two beings, a man and a woman. Eve is created as a "helpmeet opposite" (*ezer kenegdo*) to man, a part of a complete human relationship, rather than a curse. This is her *purpose*. Man does not have to continuously search for the *meaning* in each of Eve's acts.

Biblical narratives basically portray men and women as different, but in basic harmony. Eve is sent as a blessing and partner (in Hebrew, an *ezer kenegdo*, a "helpmeet opposite"), not as punishment. They will have to struggle and to work hard but can still have wonderful lives. The woman is told she will bear children in pain, but Adam also gives her the name Eve (Hebrew: *Chava*), denoting "mother of life." Adam in turn will obtain food through the sweat of his brow. Adam and Eve are now aware of their nakedness, but God signals his recognition and empathy in their new situation by giving them warm and pleasant garments to cover them. Their life may be difficult, but it is inherently *purposive.*

The biblical message in all this is far different from the message of the Greek world. Attachment is not seen as inconsistent with freedom, nor woman as a block to man's autonomy. Nor are sexual relations with a woman to be feared by man. In the biblical view there is no stigma attached to women, and sexual love is a blessing. When Genesis refers to Adam "knowing" Eve, it refers to both a physical and a spiritual knowing. The biblical term for the womb is *rehem*, which is connected to the Hebrew word *rahamim*, meaning mercy or compassion, and is a term used to describe God himself. Anything but unstable in this view, woman provides a secure base for human development. Man is not burdened with an onerous *search for meaning*, but can simply live *purposively.*

---

92. Hesiod, *Theogony*, ll. 600–610.

6. FATHERS AND SONS

A sixth contrast between the ancient Greek fixation on *searching for meaning* and the biblical emphasis of *living purposively* can be found in perhaps the two most fearsome stories in each of the respective literatures, that of Laius and Oedipus and that of Abraham and Isaac.

The Greek Narrative of Laius and Oedipus

The Greek story of Oedipus portrays the father (Laius) and the son (Oedipus) in basic conflict. King Laius of Thebes is warned by an oracle that Oedipus will kill him should he "reach man's estate" and marry his wife, Jocasta (Oedipus's natural mother).

Laius' dilemma is whether to follow the oracle's advice, given that he knows Zeus in the past has fostered father-son conflict with his own father, Cronus. Why now would Zeus be warning him about it? If Laius obeys the advice of the oracle and follows her implicit advice to sacrifice his son, will Laius avoid being displaced by his son or will he in fact bring it about? If he disobeys the advice of the oracle and does not try to sacrifice his son, will he avoid the outcome of being displaced, indeed murdered, by his son?

As the story proceeds, Laius obeys the advice of the oracle and commits the child to a herdsman with orders for his destruction. The herdsman give him to a fellowbshepherd, who carries him to King Polybus of Corinth and his queen, Meirope, by whom he is adopted and called Oedipus, or "swollen foot."

Many years later, Oedipus hears from a drunken man at a dinner party a question about his lineage. He questions Polybus and Meirope but is not satisfied by their assurances that he is their son. He immediately begins a search for his identity and goes to the oracle at Delphi (the *Pythia*) and asks her the identity of his parents. She does not answer Oedipus but gives him the same warning his biological father Laius had received: that Oedipus is destined to kill his father and marry his mother. Thinking that his foster parents are his real parents, he returns to Corinth and immediately flees the city to avoid carrying out this terrible prophecy. On the road to Thebes, at a crossroads where three roads meet, Oedipus encounters an older man in a carriage, who is blocking his way. Unbeknownst to him, the man is his biological father, Laius. A quarrel breaks out, and Oedipus slays both Laius and all but one of his attendants, and continues on his way. Shortly after, Oedipus saves Thebes from the Sphinx that was devouring passers-by by successfully answering her riddle. In gratitude for their deliverance, the

Thebans make Oedipus their king, giving him in marriage to their queen, Jocasta, who, unbeknownst to him, is his mother, thus fulfilling the very prophecy he has been trying to avoid.[93] When a pestilence falls upon Thebes, Oedipus is told that it is due to the presence within the city of the murderer of Laius. Of course, this is Oedipus himself, but he does not know this. He continues to search for clues as to the identity of the killer of Laius, ignoring his mother Jocasta's warning that he should desist.[94] Throughout this terrible story, Oedipus can be seen as driven compulsively by a *search for meaning* for the riddle of his identity that is eluding him, even if it leads to his own destruction; in this narrative, blindness (he takes out his eyes).

The Biblical Narrative of Abraham and Isaac

The biblical father-son relationship is diametrically different. A father is not the owner of his son as with the Roman *patria potestas*, nor does he hold the power of infant exposure. The father-son relationship is very different. One of the most significant themes in rabbinic literature is the command to the father to teach his children thoroughly.[95] The father's identity is not threatened by the son; he wants to see his son develop and surpass him. Yet we must address the fearsome story of the patriarch Abraham's binding of Isaac (known as the *Akedah*).

Abram's relationship with God begins when God is portrayed as telling him (Abram) to leave his father Terah's house and his pagan gods.[96] Abram leaves his father's house along with his wife, Sarai, and comes into the land of Canaan.[97] Sarai is barren; God arranges for Abram (now named Abraham) to have a son, Ishmael, with her handmaiden Hagar.[98] Later, Sarai is renamed Sarah and is given the blessing of a son, Isaac, despite her advanced age of ninety years.[99] Abraham circumcises his son Isaac when he is eight days old, as God had commanded him.[100] God will continue his covenant with God with Isaac rather than Ishmael, whom Abraham sends away at Sarah's request after Ishmael makes sport at Isaac's weaning.[101]

93. Sophocles, *Oedipus the King*.
94. Sophocles, *Oedipus the King*, ll.1059–60.
95. Deut 6:7; *b. Kiddushin*, 30a.
96. Gen 12:1–3.
97. Gen 12.
98. Gen 17:5.
99. Gen 21:1–4.
100. Gen 21:5.
101. Gen 21:8–11.

All should be well, but we are confronted with the jarring narrative of the *Akedah*—Abraham's binding of Isaac—wherein God tests Abraham by commanding him to sacrifice his son Isaac. "Take now thy son, thine only son, whom thou lovest, even Isaac and get thee into the land of Moriah; and offer him thee for burnt-offering upon one of the mountains which I will tell thee of."[102]

Abraham is prepared to go through with the sacrifice, never fully giving up hope that God will withdraw his command so that Isaac might be saved. Further, Isaac trusts in his father, despite his questioning with regard to the absence of a burnt offering. Finally, God does relent, sending an angel at the last moment to command Abraham not to sacrifice Isaac: "Lay not thine hand upon the lad."[103] When Abraham demonstrates his loyalty to God, he sends an angel to stay Abraham's hand, ending child sacrifice, which has been so prevalent in surrounding cultures. The blessing of Abraham will continue through Isaac, reaffirming the *purposive* nature of the biblical view of the father-son relationship.

The *purposive* nature of the father-son relationship is more fully expressed in the narrative of Jacob blessing his sons. Jacob, now a very old man, comes to Egypt, renews his relationship with Joseph, and makes certain that Joseph's sons, Ephraim and Manasseh, even though born in Egypt, are included within the family and are full recipients of its teachings and traditions. Finally, Jacob blesses his sons in terms of each one's unique strengths and weaknesses, affirming each as an individual personality and recognizing his unique role and creativity in the covenant. "All these are the twelve tribes of Israel, and this is what their father spoke to them. And he blessed them; he blessed each one according to his own blessing."[104]

7. MOTHERS AND DAUGHTERS

Now let us contrast living *purposively* with searching for *meaning* in an examination of the relationship between mothers and daughters. The biblical story of Naomi and Ruth provides an alternative to the Greek legend of Clytemnestra and Electra to understand the relationship between mothers and daughters as *purposive* rather than consumed with the *search for meaning*.

---

102. Gen 22.
103. Gen 22:12.
104. Gen 49:28.

The Greek Story of Clytemnestra and Electra

Electra, daughter of Agamemnon, is described as waiting for years, completely obsessed by plans for the return of her brother, Orestes, to take revenge on their mother, Clytemnestra, for her murder of her husband, Agamemnon. In a way it is *purposive*, but it is engendered by the crisis of *meaning* emerging from Electra's realization that her mother has murdered her father. The *purposiveness* of her family unit has been shattered, and Clytemnestra is obsessed with finding some *meaning* in the murder of Clytemnestra. Electra tells her mother that she has just given birth. When Clytemnestra arrives, Electra accuses her mother of cuckolding Agamemnon.[105]

Clytemnestra's response to Electra stresses the preference of the daughter for her father over her mother: "Daughter, 'twas ever thy nature to love thy father."[106] Although Electra murders her mother rather than herself, she displays her essential feeling of debasement as a woman: "Ah me! Alas! And whither can I go? . . . What husband will accept me as his bride?"[107] Electra's *purposiveness* as a woman has been shattered and she is driven in despair to look for an alternate *meaning* structure, as destructive as it may be.

The Biblical Story of Naomi and Ruth

The biblical book of Ruth portrays a very different view of mother-daughter relationships. Naomi had moved with her prosperous husband and two sons from Bethlehem in Judah to Moab. There Naomi's husband has died, and the sons also die after marrying Moabite women—Orpah and Ruth. Bereft of both family and wealth, Naomi determines to return to Bethlehem. Orpah and Ruth insists on accompanying her. As much as Naomi could benefit from the support and companionship of two young women, she nevertheless unselfishly urges them to return to their families of origin in Moab. Orpah leaves but Ruth stays with Naomi, who still seeks to persuade her to leave. Ruth replies with one of the most beautiful speeches in the Bible.

> Entreat me not to leave thee, or to return from following after thee: for whither thou goest, I will go; and where thou lodgest, I will lodge: thy people shall be my people, and thy God my God . . .[108]

---

105. Sophocles, *Oedipus the King*, ll.1063–99.
106. Sophocles, *Oedipus the King*, ll. 1102–5.
107. Sophocles, *Oedipus the King*, ll. 1200–202.
108. Ruth 1:16–17.

Ruth's good character and her kindness to Naomi become known in Bethlehem and attract the notice of Boaz, a wealthy and dignified community leader, and a kinsman of Naomi's late husband. Naomi helped facilitate a match between Ruth and Boaz to give Ruth "a resting place which will be good for her."[109] Ruth remains devoted to her former mother-in-law, who has acted so unselfishly toward her. Boaz marries Ruth, and in due course a son is born. Naomi becomes the nurse, taking the infant into her arms. The women of Bethlehem affirm her joy, saying, "There is a son is born to Naomi."[110] It is not just any son, but Obed, who is "the father of Jesse, the father of David."[111] Ruth is fulfilling her *purposiveness* as a daughter, a wife, and a mother, and is not driven in a compulsive search for *meaning* which drives Electra.

8. SIBLINGS

Both the Hebrew Bible and the literature of ancient Greece present stories of family conflict. However, several basic difference between these literatures can be quickly noted. The stories of Genesis abound with sibling conflict, portraying sons vying for paternal approval and blessing. Although the sons are competitive, they are *purposive* in terms of aiming to be their father's successor. The earliest myths of ancient Greece are very different, portraying conflict between father and son rather than between brothers, with the brothers often banding together, joined by the mother to kill or castrate the menacing father. The biblical sense of intergenerational *purpose* is absent and is replaced by a fierce competition in a search for *meaning*.[112] Each brother is trying to prevail, but with no family *purpose*.

This difference can be illustrated by examining whether sibling conflict can be resolved. The Hebrew Bible offers a plan to resolve family conflict through the *purposive* nature of the father's blessing. Originally the source of the sibling conflict, the blessing may work to achieve some level of reconciliation between his sons, as in Jacob's blessings to all his sons, giving each of them a *purpose*. Greek literature offers no such balm, never developing the idea that a father should bless his children. The result is that conflict in the families grows angrier and nastier in each succeeding generation until the families self-destruct, as does the family of Oedipus.

---

109. Ruth 3:1.
110. Ruth 4:14–15.
111. Ruth 4:17.
112. See the historical reconstruction by Sigmund Freud in *Totem and Taboo*.

The Greek Sibling Pattern

Four examples of the Greek family pattern come to mind: a) Cronus and his brothers, b) Zeus and his brothers, c) Heracles and Iphicles, and d) Eteocles and Polyneices. In all of these stories, the sons do not seem to be inheriting anything from their fathers:

A. Uranus is angry over the birth of the offspring and he shoves them back into his wife, Gaia, as they are born. The offspring are artificially united by a common enemy, their father. Groaning with pains, Gaia instigated their son Cronus to castrate Uranus and overthrow his rule.[113]

B. Cronus then repeats his father's pattern, imprisoning his brothers, the Titans, in Tartarus. He then marries his sister, Rhea, and, fearful of the prophecy of Earth and Sky (his parents) that he will lose his rule to his own son, he devours his offspring as they are born.[114] Only Zeus escapes through a ruse on the part of his mother—"she wrapped a stone in swaddling clothes and gave it to Cronus to swallow as though it were the infant (Zeus) which had just been born."[115]

Ultimately, Cronus is given a drink that forces him to vomit out the children he had swallowed (Zeus's siblings) and, together, Zeus and his siblings wage war against Cronus and the Titans. Zeus only becomes victorious, however, when he allies with the Titans against Cronus.[116]

C. A third example of the relationship between paternal threat and sibling rivalry can be seen in the narrative of Heracles and Iphicles. Although the two boys are described as twins born from the same mother, they have different fathers.[117] As the power of Zeus wanes, rivalry between the young males emerges in earnest, encouraged by Zeus's wife, Hera.

D. Consider now the family of Oedipus himself—in relation to his sons rather than to his father. When the horrible truth of the incestuous union between Oedipus and his mother becomes known, Jocasta kills herself and Oedipus takes out his eyes. His sons, Eteocles and Polyneices, who were to share the power of Thebes, abandon their now powerless father. They allow him to be exiled from Thebes and he

---

113. Apollodorus, *Library* 1.1.
114. Apollodorus, *Library* 1.1.5.
115. Apollodorus, *Library* 1.1–7.
116. Apollodorus, *Library* 2.4.12.
117. Apollodorus, *Library* 2.4.8.

wanders alone, cared for by his daughters. Before his death, Oedipus announces a curse that his sons should die by each other's hands.[118]

As any sense of *purpose* in the father-son relationship is absent, and sibling rivalry increases with the declining powers of the father.

The Biblical Sibling Pattern

Consider in contrast the stories of (a) Cain and Abel, (b) Isaac and Ishmael, (c) Jacob and Esau, and d) Joseph and his brothers. These four generations display a decrease of the pathology of sibling rivalry with an increase in paternal blessing.

A. God gives blessings directly to Adam and Eve[119] and to Noah and his family.[120] But there is no indication that God blesses Cain and Abel directly or that Adam gives either son a blessing. A direct blessing by Adam to his sons, showing each his place in the larger divine *purpose*, might well have prevented the murder of one sibling, Abel, by the other, Cain.

B. Abraham circumcises both Ishmael[121] and Isaac.[122] According to some interpretations (Rabbi Nehamiah), Abraham gives his blessing only to Isaac, though others (Rabbi Hama) interpret Abraham as giving only gifts to Isaac.[123] Subsequently, Sarah demands that Abraham send Ishmael and his mother Hagar out into the desert because of his mocking Isaac at a feast celebrating Isaac's weaning (at least this provided Sarah with an excuse).[124] At the same time, Abraham apparently has become close to Ishmael after a period of estrangement[125] and both sons join together in burying Abraham in the cave of Machpelah. Isaac and Ishmael do seem to be able to cooperate when necessary, and one does not kill the other.

C. God first tells Rebecca when she is still pregnant that Jacob and Esau will be two great nations in her womb and that the older will serve

---

118. Sophocles, *Oedipus at Colonus*, 1386-94; Aeschylus, *Seven against Thebes*, 879-924.

119. Gen 1:28

120. Gen 9:1.

121. Gen 16:22.

122. Gen 21:21.

123. Gen. Rab. 61:6; Rashi on Gen 25:9.

124. Gen 21:9

125. Gen 25:9

the younger.[126] God subsequently does bless Jacob (the younger),[127] but does not seem specifically to bless Esau. Isaac does bless Jacob[128] and then Esau,[129] giving each son a blessing that may be suitable for him. Esau naturally hates Jacob because he feels his blessing is stolen from him and so threatens to kill Jacob.[130] But with the intervention of the mother, Rebecca, peace between the brothers is restored and ultimately Esau indicates satisfaction with his portion.[131]

D. Jacob experiences the joy of seeing his sons reconciled despite their many problems with both him and each other. Even the selling of Joseph comes to a happy ending when Joseph as viceroy of Egypt saves the family from famine in so wise a manner that the old wounds are appreciably healed. There is no mention of a direct blessing given by God to Jacob's sons. However, in his last moments, Jacob conscientiously and lovingly blessed his sons, each according to his own personality and his own needs.[132] Going a step further, Jacob also blesses his grandsons, Ephraim and Manasseh.[133]

In summary, then, we argue that the greater incidence of sibling rivalry in narratives in Genesis than in Greek mythology is misleading. It is a function of the underlying *purposiveness* of the biblical family—the sons competing to inherit the covenant of the father. The father's blessing can resolve this rivalry as culminated in Jacob's blessing to all his sons. Strikingly, his sense of *purpose* allows him to see each of his sons uniquely and give a unique blessing to each one.

The Greek family, in contrast, is *purposeless*. The father is not a source of inheritance but is an impediment. Sibling rivalry is initially masked by the threat of the father to the sons, who must band together to protect themselves. However, this bonding is shallow and will disappear as the paternal threat recedes, and the *search for meaning* intensifies. This pattern is consummated in the curse of Oedipus to his two sons to slay each other.

---

126. Gen 25:23–24.
127. Gen 25:24, 28:14, 32:30.
128. Gen 27:27–30.
129. Gen 31:39–40.
130. Gen 27:41.
131. Gen 33.
132. Gen 49.
133. Gen 48:21.

9. SELF AND OTHER

The Greek Story of Narcissus

The terms "narcissism" and "narcissistic" have become almost bromides in modern society to describe people who are extremely selfish and self-involved. The actual story of Narcissus provides a much richer picture, ending in his suicide. It describes a person without self-knowledge and *purpose*.

The earliest sources of the myth of Narcissus have long since been lost. Our most complete account from antiquity is in Ovid's *Metamorphoses* (ca. 43 BCE to 17 CE). Narcissus is born out of the rape of his mother, Lirope, by a river god. When Lirope enquires from the Greek seer Tiresias about whether her son will live to a ripe old age, she receives a strange answer: "He [Narcissus] will live a long life as long as he doesn't come to know himself."[134] He will only live to the extent that he has no self-knowledge and thus exists *without purpose*.

Narcissus grows to be a vain young man, so physically beautiful that many fall in love with him by simply looking at him.[135] Narcissus, however, is totally self-absorbed, *searching for meaning* to fill the emptiness in his soul, and treating lovers of both sexes as mere mirrors of himself. Echo, the nymph who loves Narcissus in vain, is transformed, left merely repeating the words he says—as an echo.[136] One would-be lover who feels scorned prays to the god of fate, Nemesis, and asks that Narcissus too fall hopelessly in love and be unable to achieve his desire.[137] Soon, Narcissus sees a beautiful youth in a pond, not realizing it is his own reflection. Narcissus is obsessed with the image in the brook, and looks at it night and day.[138]

Ultimately, however, Narcissus recognizes the face in the brook is simply his own reflection.[139] Such a psychotic juxtaposition rips Narcissus apart. As Ovid expresses it, "How I wish I could separate myself from my body."[140] Narcissus finally becomes aware of the unobtainability of the figure he sees in the pond—searching for a *meaning* that is missing in his *purposeless* life. Since he does not know himself, his life has no *purpose*. Narcissus pines away until he dies, mourning the youth he loves in vain.

---

134. Ovid, *Metamorphoses* 3.343–50.
135. Ovid, *Metamorphoses* 3.343–50, 359–78.
136. Ovid, *Metamorphoses* 3.379–382.
137. Ovid, *Metamorphoses* 3.405–6.
138. Ovid, *Metamorphoses* 3.414–54.
139. Ovid, *Metamorphoses* 3.463–73.
140. Ovid, *Metamorphoses* 3.468–69.

This ends in his death, described in Ovid[141] as pining away, and in Conon as actively stabbing himself in his chest.[142]

The Biblical Story of Jonah

The biblical story of Jonah is dramatically different. Jonah has a *purpose*; he is called upon by God to go to the people of Nineveh and warn them to repent of their wickedness. Jonah tries to evade his *purpose* and flees to Tarshish. But God will not let him avoid his *purpose* and sends a great storm to threaten the ship that Jonah is on. Jonah first tries to hide from his *purpose* by sleeping in the bottom of the ship.[143] But ultimately his identity as a Hebrew is revealed and he tells his shipmates that he is a Hebrew[144] and to throw him overboard so they can save themselves.[145] The story could thus end in Jonah's death, but it doesn't—God intervenes as a protective parent, swallowing Jonah in the protective stomach of a great fish until he overcomes his confusion. While Jonah is in the belly of the fish, he prays to God, reaffirming his *purpose*. After three days, the fish vomits Jonah out safely onto dry land:

Then Jonah prays to the Lord his God from the fish's belly:

> For You cast me into the depth, into the heart of the seas, and the floods surrounded me; all Your billows and Your waves passed over me. Then I said: 'I have been cast out of Your sight'; yet I will look again toward Your holy temple . . . I will pay what I have vowed. Salvation is of the Lord." So the Lord spoke to the fish, and it vomited Jonah onto dry land.[146]

Once again, God commands Jonah to go to Nineveh. This time Jonah fulfills his *purpose* and gives the people of Nineveh God's message. They repent and are saved.[147] Jonah is angry, however, and desires to die: "But it displeased Jonah exceedingly, and he became angry . . . 'Therefore now, O Lord, please take my life from me; for it is better for me to die than to live!'"[148]

---

141. Ovid, *Metamorphoses* 3.497–500.
142. Conon, *Narrationes*, 24.
143. Jonah 1:5.
144. Jonah 1:7–10.
145. Jonah 11–16.
146. Jonah 2.
147. Jonah 3:1–10.
148. Jonah 4:1–3.

Jonah leaves the city to sit at its outskirts under a burning sun.[149] There he is shielded by a gourd plant that God makes to grow up over him.

> And the Lord God prepared a plant and made it come up over Jonah, that it might be a shade for his head to deliver him from his misery. Again, God intervenes, sheltering Jonah with a leafy bush from the burning sun. So Jonah was very grateful for the plant.[150]

After a worm destroys the protective bush, Jonah again expresses suicidal thoughts.[151] God intervenes, this time engaging Jonah in a dialogue reinforcing Jonah's *purpose* of saving the people of Nineveh.[152]

Table 6. Jonah against Narcissus		
Stage	Narcissus	Jonah
1. Precipitating stressor	Narcissus is born of a rape of his mother. He is prophesied to have a long life as long as "he does not come to know himself."	God asks Jonah to go and warn the wicked people of Nineveh to repent and avoid great punishment. Jonah does not want to go and boards a ship to Tarshish to avoid the conflict.
2. Reaction	The beautiful Narcissus heartlessly exhibits hubris by rejecting would-be lovers of both genders.	God sends a great storm and Jonah tries to hide his identity. However, his identity as a Hebrew is discovered. He tells his shipmates that he is the reason for the storm and asks them to throw him overboard. However, rather than let him drown, God sends a big fish to swallow Jonah and protect him, allowing him to recover his strength, and come to "know himself."
3. Response of others	Narcissus is brought down by Nemesis and becomes completely infatuated with a face he encounters in a brook.	After the fish vomits out the restored Jonah onto dry land, God again asks him to go to Nineveh to warn its inhabitants to repent and change their ways. This time Jonah goes.

---

149. Jonah 4:1–4.
150. Jonah 4:6.
151. Jonah 4:7–8.
152. Jonah 4:9–11.

4. Effect	Narcissus realizes the face in the brook is his, and thus unobtainable. He is without an identity, which self-knowledge makes possible. He commits suicide, either in a passive (pining away) or active (stabbing himself) manner, depending on the source. Narcissus obsessively looks to the outside world for his own missing identity, for *meaning*. Yet, according to prophesy, if he finds it, he will die.	Jonah warns the people of Nineveh but becomes suicidal again and sits outside the city walls under a hot sun. God again protects Jonah by shielding him from the sun with a large gourd. Ultimately, God removes the gourd and, in addressing Jonah's complaint, strengthens Jonah's identity and teaches him the lesson of mercy and compassion—and that reaching out to others *purposively* does not mean that he has to lose himself.

Significantly, the difference between these two narratives is reflected in a comparison of Jewish law and Anglo-American law with regard to *Good Samaritan* responses to people in difficulty in three different areas: a) return of lost property, b) rendering aid, and c) coming to the rescue of someone in danger. With regard to return of lost property, the two systems seem similar. However, a comparison of Jewish and American law with respect to rendering aid and coming to the rescue of someone in danger suggests that Jewish law encourages a duty to help in a manner unusual under Anglo-American law.

Nevertheless, this difference has become somewhat muted over time, with a number of states enacting Good Samaritan statutes. As long as these statutes are specific in terms of duties and liabilities to be imposed, society may benefit from them without incurring restraints on individual liberties.[153]

10. WAR AND PEACE

The tenth and final section of this chapter offers a contrast between ancient Greek and biblical views of peace and war and soldiering. Wars always involve violence, suffering, and death, often of innocent people. Yet biblical and ancient Greek views on warfare differ notably.

In the Greek historian Herodotus' view, the gods are capricious as well as having limited power. Ancient Greek epics like the *Iliad* seem to admire violence as an end in itself. They delight in describing in gory detail the slaughter on the battlefield, totally disconnected to any transcendent

---

153. Besser and Kaplan, *Good Samaritan*.

purpose.[154] Wars in the Bible can also be very violent and destructive, for example, in describing the exploits of some of David's best warriors.[155] Yet war is not glorified for its own sake. Wars are fought at best under certain guidelines and for aims that the Bible describes, largely to achieve God's purposes for human history. On some occasions, the Bible will mandate the destruction of a culture that has deviated too far from morally acceptable behavior. Yet this seems fundamentally unlike the picture of fighting in ancient epics like the *Iliad*, in which violence seems to be admired as an end in itself and which delight in describing in gory detail the slaughter on the battlefield, totally disconnected to any transcendent purpose. As a case in point, let us compare the epic battles of Achilles and Hector with that of David and Goliath.

The Greek Story of Achilles and Hector

The Trojan Hector is described by Homer as a family man, very human and aware of his obligations to his family and to society. He has serious doubts about the behavior of his brother Paris in abducting Helen from her husband, King Menelaus of Sparta, thus instigating the war, but Hector does nothing about it. Unlike David, Hector is terrified of his much stronger adversary, Achilles.

Achilles is described in superhuman terms and as invulnerable, except for his heel. He is moody and ferocious as a warrior and seems to express himself through violence. When the mortally wounded Hector proposes that the victor treat the vanquished's body with respect, Achilles angrily refuses, saying that he only wishes he could bring himself to eat Hector's body. The Achaean soldiers stab and mock Hector's corpse. Then Achilles ties the body to his chariot and drags it around the walls of Troy, where the Trojans can see it.[156]

The Biblical Story of David and Goliath

Goliath is described as "six cubits and a span" tall, perhaps over nine feet. His armor alone weighs five thousand shekels. Descriptions of armor are not the norm in Scriptures in contrast to Homer's detailed description of

---

154. Herodotus, *Histories* 14.
155. 2 Sam 22.
156. Homer, *Iliad* 22.

Achilles' armor in the *Iliad*. David, in contrast, is a young shepherd with no armor, carrying a staff, a shepherd's pouch, and a sling with five stones.[157]

The description of the combat itself further confirms the difference between the two protagonists. Goliath is a warrior from his youth who flaunts the Israelites with a personal challenge which he knows no one will accept. It is all a ploy to demoralize the Israelite army, and it is highly successful. For forty days, every morning and evening, the giant comes forth and offers the same challenge, mocking the Israelites and their God. The outcome would be up to God, but someone has to try. Though young, David is a person of deep faith that God will do what he wants. David goes out quickly to meet Goliath, carrying his sling with five stones and an ability to use them expertly. Goliath seems surprised and shaken. David seizes the right moment and fires a stone into Goliath's forehead, killing him. He then completes his astonishing victory by severing Goliath's head, at which the Philistines flee in panic, and the Israelites pursue them vigorously.[158]

A number of points should be noted in this story. First, violence is not glorified, nor is brute strength. Goliath is experienced, well armed, and huge. David moves swiftly. More important, Goliath has no goal higher than just fighting, while David feels he is fighting for a higher *purpose*.

A Comparison of Biblical and Greek Approaches to War and Peace

We have discussed two narratives comparing biblical and Greek views of war and peace. While the Greek accounts may have a particular meaning, they do not seem to have any transcendent purpose. Let us compare these two bedrock cultures over nine basic categories with respect to our larger question of a transcendent sense of *purpose* versus a search for *meaning*.

1. Precipitation of the conflict: While the biblical world seems to want to avoid conflict if possible, the ancient Greek world seems to relish in it. Everything seems to be a competition in Greek thinking. A wins *only* if B loses.[159]
2. Purpose of the conflict: Biblical stories emphasize that war must be conducted in terms of God's plan for history. Greek wars are typically not fought in terms of any divine plan for history.

---

157. 1 Sam 17:38–40.
158. 1 Sam 42–54.
159. Gouldner, *Enter Plato*.

3. Actions towards the environment: Greek armies typically destroy the environment while biblical armies are forbidden by biblical law to destroy fruit trees.
4. Glorification of violence: While the biblical world is certainly not passive and will wage serious war, there seems to be little love of violence in itself. The ancient Greek mindset seems to be inherently competitive and to enjoy war for war's sake. The biblical mindset is willing to wage war in terms of defense of the biblical way of life.
5. Flexibility of the military: While the Greek approach to battle often seems to involve a fairly stationary test of brute strength and numbers, the biblical approach typically seems to depend on flexibility and a sense of transcendent purpose. Military battles are fought for a reason, not just as a test of strength or from a sense of duty.
6. Willingness to physically destroy the enemy: While both the biblical and ancient Greek mindsets seem willing to completely annihilate the enemy, the reasons are different. The Greek mindset seems to enjoy the battle and inflicting severe pain upon one's adversary. The biblical mindset, in contrast, does not focus on violence, but is willing to use violence to destroy nations who are attacking the Israelite covenant with God.
7. Preference for peace over war: The biblical mindset, while willing to engage in war, seems to prefer a more peaceful, cooperative solution if possible. The Greek mindset seems to actually enjoy physical conflict as a form of competition.
8. Depiction of military heroes: While the ancient Greeks often seem to idealize military heroes, the biblical mindset is more mixed. While honoring military achievement, the biblical attitude points more to peace. The Greek mindset seems to love conflict.
9. Perception of the human being: The Greeks continuously search for life meaning through grandiosity, often involving military glory. The Israelites, in contrast, believe that man is inherently an exalted being created in the image of God himself, and is not to seek glory but to live according to God's instructions.

In summary then, this chapter has attempted to contrast biblical and ancient Greek attitudes in ten areas of life.

9

Biblical versus Greek Prophecy

Living Purposively against Searching for Meaning

LET US CONCLUDE THIS book with an examination of how differently prophecy is viewed in the biblical and Greek worlds, and the implications of this difference with regard to living *purposively* versus obsessively searching for *meaning*. In the Greek world, prophecy is deterministic, and cannot be avoided. *Outcome Y will occur and cannot be avoided.* There is no saving antecedent X. The human being is propelled in a fruitless search for *meaning*, for that X, if you will. There is no *meaning* to be found, because nothing can really change. Even when the Trojan prophetess Cassandra, daughter of Priam and Hecuba, warns the Trojans to beware of the horse the Greeks are leaving outside Troy (and are hiding inside of), no one will listen to her.[1]

The biblical world has a completely differing view of prophecy. Here heeding prophetic warnings can allow the human being to change what happens to him. This is indeed the basis of social intervention. *Outcome Y will occur unless antecedent X intervenes.* In the book of Jonah, the people of Nineveh will be destroyed—unless they repent. But it is the possibility of the saving antecedent X that gives the Hebrew Bible an inspiring therapeutic vision rather than a tragic one, and this possibility of change, indeed repentance. The rejection of fatalism is what makes the biblical prophet Nathan a

---

1. When Cassandra rejects Apollo's embrace, she is punished by being able to prophesy but not having her prophecies believed (Hyginus, *Fabulae* 93).

concerned messenger of God rather than a taunting actuary like the Greek prophet Teiresias. If the biblical prophet is successful in his endeavors, then his dire predictions will not come to pass. His statements are *purposeful*.

DEVELOPMENT VERSUS CYCLE: ECCLESIASTES AGAINST SISYPHUS

As way of illustration, let us compare the Greek story of Sisyphus with the book of Ecclesiastes (*Koheleth*) in the Hebrew Scriptures.

Sisyphus, Cycle and Meaninglessness

The Greek legend of Sisyphus is essentially as follows.

> Sisyphos son of Aiolos founded the city of Ephyra (which is now called Corinth) and married Merope, daughter of Atlas. They had a son, Glaucos, who with Eurymede had a son, Bellerophontes, who killed the fire-breathing Chimaira. Sysiphos is punished in Hades' Realm by rolling a boulder with his hands and head, wanting to force it over the top. But when the stone is about to be forced over by him, it forces its way back down again. He pays this penalty because of Asopos' daughter Algina. For when Asopos was looking for her, it is said, Sisyphos revealed to him that Zeus had secretly taken her away.[2]

Camus employs this legend to illustrate his view of life without *meaning*. Man is burdened by a grandiose need to avoid any limitations on his power or freedom. The world is alien and threatening. *Hubris* will end in *nemesis*. No amount of heroic activity or achievement can transcend this reality, the onset of nemesis. Yet his failures only deepen the trap.[3] Camus's Sisyphus continuously pushes the aforementioned huge rock up a hill, only for it to crash down on him. He tries again with the same result. Ultimately, death is the only freedom. And since everyone dies at the end, life is essentially *meaningless*. Yet the human being is trapped in this endlessly cyclical and futile *search for meaning*. Camus goes even further, raising the question of suicide.

---

2. Apollodorus. *Library* 1.85

3. It is noteworthy that Sisyphus carries his burden alone: he has no companion, no friend, no sweetheart, and no family with him.

The fundamental subject of *The Myth of Sisyphus* is this: it is legitimate and necessary to wonder whether life has a meaning; therefore, it is legitimate to meet the problem of suicide face to face.[4]

Ecclesiastes (Koheleth), Development and Purpose

The biblical book of Ecclesiastes (*Koheleth*, "the preacher") rejects the pattern of the cycle that is inherent in the myth of Sisyphus. Koheleth asks searching questions, as does Camus, but here the cycle is merely a problem with which to deal, not the all-determining basis of human existence. Koheleth's world is neither meaningless nor absurd, and in it humans may work, learn, and be happy. Let us look at Koheleth's rejection of the cycle design, a rejection shared by later rabbinic thought.

Indeed, Koheleth does indeed speak of cycles early in the first chapter:

> What profit has a man from all his labor in which he toils under the sun?
> One generation passes away, and another generation comes; but the earth abides forever.
> The sun also rises, and the sun goes down, And hastens to the place where it arose.
> The wind goes toward the south, and turns about to the north; the wind whirls about continually, and comes again on its circuit.
> All the rivers run into the sea, yet the sea is not full; to the place from which the rivers come, there they return again.[5]

This is the cycle of seasons: one might call it the "ecological cycle." However, it is not a deterministic cycle of nations or of human lives, and it is not the product of some mystical fate. It is the same pattern that God establishes to reassure Noah after the great flood, a gracious gift to man and not a chafing burden. This pattern sets certain parameters for human activity and wisdom, but it does not foredoom the individual or greatly limit his ability to be useful, productive, or content. There is no indication that the preacher, Koheleth, sees this natural cycle as nefarious or threatening.

The famous third chapter, in contrast, seems to indicate a concept of development with regard to human affairs:

> To everything there is a season, a time for every purpose under heaven:
> A time to be born, and a time to die;

---

4. Camus, *Myth of Sisyphus*, Preface.
5. Eccl 1:3–7.

> A time to plant, and a time to pluck what is planted; A time to kill, and a time to heal;
> A time to break down, and a time to build up; A time to weep, and a time to laugh;
> A time to mourn, and a time to dance;
> A time to cast away stones, and a time to gather stones;
> A time to embrace, and a time to refrain from embracing; A time to gain, and a time to lose;
> A time to keep, and a time to throw away; A time to tear, and a time to sew;
> A time to keep silence, and a time to speak; A time to love, and a time to hate;
> A time of war, and a time of peace.[6]

The above passage does not describe life as a cycle. Rather, it advises that there is a time for everything. Some situations may require planting, and other situations uprooting; there is a time to be born and a time to die. Indeed, many things that come from God are beyond human reach, but humans do not need to feel helpless or doomed. Recognizing mortal limitations and accepting divine omnipotence does not threaten the individual with annihilation.[7]

Koheleth faces a dilemma, as does the Greek tragic hero; but the key question is not whether the individual should go on living in a world that has no use for him. Koheleth is not touched by suicidal doubts. Rather, since the world functions so well, he wonders what is left for humans to improve or create. "What profit has a man from all his labor in which he toils under the sun? . . . There is nothing new under the sun. Is there any- thing of which it may be said, 'See this is new'? It has already been in ancient times before us."[8] This is not a mere academic exercise; it is a deeply troubling question. Yet, while an ultimate answer is not to be found, there is enough to do in the meantime, and Koheleth seeks to learn, to understand, and to do. "And I set my heart to seek and search out by wisdom concerning all that is done under heaven."[9] Wisdom can indeed increase both human sensitivity and human pain: "For in much wisdom is much grief."[10] But wisdom is still a good thing: "Then I saw that wisdom excels folly as light excels darkness."[11]

---

6 Eccl 3:1–8.
7. See Kaplan and Schwartz, *Psychology of Hope*, 65–71.
8. Eccl 1:3–10.
9. Eccl 1:17.
10. Eccl 1:18
11. Eccl 2:13.

There is no suggestion here, as there is in Sophocles' *Oedipus*, that human wisdom's truest value lies in making people feel their misery.[12] Misery is miserable, not sublime. Humans need not feel impelled toward a pitiable fate; they need not live in the rarefied yet horrifying pattern of tragic heroes, of Prometheus and Antigone. Humans can enjoy life, and God sees this as good. "There is nothing better for a man than that he should eat and drink, and that his soul should enjoy good in his labor. This also, I saw, was from the hand of God."[13]

In contrast to Sisyphus, Koheleth contends that a person should not live alone. Association with others can be frustrating, and yet he says, "Live joyfully with the wife whom you love."[14] And he continues: "The three-fold cord is not quickly severed."[15] One cannot be totally egocentric. Koheleth opposes many aspects and implications of the cyclical-heroic view. Camus rejects a belief in God and any notion of human immortality; indeed, he sees in this rejection of God the basis of human freedom. Koheleth affirms that man is by nature morally free and able to reach some sort of accommodation with God. The problem is not God, nor the universe, nor humankind. Instead, there exists the practical question of what humans may do that will make a difference.

Camus sees Sisyphus's realization of his misery as his nirvana, the whole meaning of his being. Koheleth prizes wisdom, but not as the sole value or as effective without the body. Koheleth is troubled by the very real dilemma of misery that is caused by factors beyond man's power. But this is not the only issue in life, and one need not completely despair if one cannot resolve it. In any case, some miseries are within human power to remedy. Koheleth does not depict the world as alternating starkly between the two poles of hubris and nemesis, success and failure, all or nothing. The question is not life versus suicide, "to be or not to be." Given that there is life and there is death, the question is how humans should react. There is no fencing with the illusion of a final answer. Rabbi Tarfon declared very succinctly centuries later: "It is not thy duty to complete the work but neither mayest thou desist from it."[16]

---

12. Sophocles, *Oedipus the King* 1.335.
13. Eccl 2:24.
14. Eccl 9:9.
15. Eccl 4:12.
16. BT *Mishna Avot*, 2.16. Rabbinic literature does, in fact, contain the notion that the world was not created in a perfect state and that man may and should improve it; for example, "Everything that was created in the first six days needs improvement" (Pesikta Rabbati, 23). See also Soloveitchik, *Halakhic Man*.

The difference between these two points of view are graphically illustrated in the stories of Narcissus and Jonah, discussed in the previous chapter, which offer contrasting models of individual development. The myth of Narcissus depicts a chilling tale of wasteful cyclical self-disintegration; by contrast, the book of Jonah offers a compelling analysis of the developmental struggle toward self-integration and maturation.[17]

PUTTING TIME INTO THE SYLLOGISM

Critical to this difference between Israel and Hellas is the contrast between the cyclical and developmental view of human life and their contrasting views of time, stasis, and change in the Greek and biblical worlds. Plato experienced a number of changes that may have been quite devastating to him, including the breakdown of the Athenian state, and specifically the trial and execution of his mentor, Socrates. Perhaps this is why Plato elevates *being* over *becoming* as a higher form of knowledge. As *being* is to *becoming*, so *knowledge* is to *opinion*. The glue of the Greek world, then, is *stasis* (always in an uneasy battle with *chaos*) and life is a static riddle reduced to a search for *meaning*. Change is a threat to this equilibrium and thus life is devoid of *purpose*.[18] By tradition, Plato was said to have engraved over the door to his academy the phrase: "Let no one ignorant of geometry come under my roof."[19]

Biblical society views time very differently. It embraces change and the future. God's response to Moses asking for his name, *ehiyeh asher ehiyeh*.[20] This answer is given in first-person singular imperfect form, ancient Hebrew lacking a future tense, but is probably best translated as "I will be what I will be," given the context of God promising to be with his people through their future troubles. The glue of the biblical world is the Creator. Thus, change is not threatening, and the future need not be dreaded, nor *meaning*

---

17. A striking exception to this closed Greek view can be found in the exchange between Agamemnon, the head of the Greek forces in Troy, and Odysseus with regard to disposition of Ajax's body after he has killed himself. Fixated on Ajax's enmity toward both of them after Agamemnon had conferred the armor of the slain hero Achilles on Odysseus, Agamemnon intends to leave Ajax's body unburied, a dishonor in Greek society. When Odysseus protests, stating that he wishes to bury Ajax's body, Agamemnon is stunned, saying, "Thou, Odysseus, champion him (Ajax) against me?" Odysseus responds, "Yes, I hated him when hate was honorable" (Sophocles, *Ajax* 1346–49).

18. Plato, *Republic*, 7.514a—7.521d.
19. Tzetzes, *Chiliades* 8.973.
20. Exod 3:14.

BIBLICAL VERSUS GREEK PROPHECY

obsessively searched for as an abstract entity dystonic to the person himself. Life is seen as dynamic and thus *purposive*.

Consider the standard Aristotelian syllogism, containing a major premise, a minor premise, and a conclusion. For example:

1. All men are mortal. (Major premise)
2. Socrates is a man. (Minor premise)
3. Therefore, Socrates is mortal. (Conclusion)

Let us apply this Greek syllogistic reasoning to the biblical story of the Israelites coming out of Egypt:

1. No persons who are slaves can enter into the "promised land." (Major premise)
2. All Israelites coming out of Egypt are slaves. (Minor premise)
3. Therefore, no Israelite can enter the "promised land." (Conclusion)

However, according to the biblical account, this is not what happens. Or, more to the point, this is what happens initially, as no persons of the "slave generation" are allowed to enter the "promised land." However, after forty years, descendants coming out of Egypt are considered free enough emotionally and cognitively from a "slave mentality" to be allowed to come into the "promised land." And it is this awareness of time itself— the passage of time, to be exact—that transforms the closed, static, overdetermined Greek syllogism into an open, dynamic, *purposeful* assertion of freedom and belief in change and development.

A biblical conception of the above syllogism can be represented as follows:

1. No persons who have the mentality of slaves can enter into the "promised land." (Major premise)
2. All Israelites coming out of Egypt initially have the mentality of slaves. (Minor premise)
3. Therefore, no Israelite can initially enter into the "promised land" while he has that "slave mentality." (Initial conclusion)
4. However, after forty years in the desert, a new generation of Israelites is born who do not carry this slave mentality from Egypt. (Adjusted premise)
5. Therefore, after forty years, the Israelites are allowed to enter into the "promised land." (Adjusted conclusion)

In other words, the Hebrew idea of a syllogism is dynamic and *purposeful*. Why? Because it is not static. To employ Plato's language, it values *becoming* over *being*. Time is the salvific element missing in the Greek worldview, certainly the Platonic one. In the words of Norwegian clergyman and noted linguist Thorlief Boman, Greek thinking emphasizes the observable, the static, the logical, and the nomothetic, while in contradistinction, Hebrew thought stresses hearing, the dynamic, the psychological, and the ideographic.[21]

More recently, Yosef Yersushalmi continued in the same vein, arguing that Freud himself carried the Greek cyclical view of history and sense of hopelessness into the very fabric of psychoanalysis. As a result, Freud's approach was fundamentally constrained by a Greek-based narrative *meaning* structure that failed to offer practitioners and patients alike an ambitious vision of psychological well-being.[22] I have suggested that psychotherapy would benefit from a biblical counternarrative emphasizing *purposiveness*.

Finally, biblical characters do not face the same "Hobson's Choices" that Greek heroes do. They are not presented with riddling sphinxes and oracles that distort their sense of judgment. Even when they do seem to be mired in no-win situations, there is typically a stopper, an opportunity to return to their covenant to deepen their relationship with God. In short, the Bible is not a Greek tragedy. Time is the element that converts a riddle into a parable, and a futile search for *meaning* into a *purposeful* life.

THE ENTRAPMENT OF THE RIDDLE

A vivid example of how trapped a person can become in a fatalistic world is provided in my recently published two-act play, *Oedipus in Jerusalem*.[23] In this play, the biblical prophet Nathan meets the blinded Oedipus wandering alone outside of Thebes. Nathan becomes convinced Oedipus is innocent of the crimes of intentional patricide and incest, as he didn't know the identity of either his father or mother and actively attempted to avoid committing these crimes. Nathan brings Oedipus for trial to the Sanhedrin in Jerusalem, with the Greek playwright Sophocles serving as accuser and Nathan himself serving as the defender of Oedipus, who insists he is guilty.

The Sanhedrin acquits Oedipus, concluding he has been done in by "fate," which actually is nothing magical at all but the result of incomplete information, misleading riddles, and confusing statements, leaving Oedipus without accurate knowledge of his situation and thus entrapping him. A dialogue between Nathan and the Oracle of Delphi indicts Greek thinking

21. Boman, *Hebrew Thought Compared to Greek*.
22. Yerushalmi, *Freud's Moses*.
23. Kaplan, *Oedipus in Jerusalem*.

as representing an abstract geometrical concoction rather than the organic morality inherent in biblical thinking. Oedipus is reprimanded for only one act, destroying his eyes, a prohibited self-mutilation in the Bible and Jewish law.[24] Oedipus, thoroughly indoctrinated by Greek thinking, refuses to accept the verdict of innocence, shouting that he is the "worst of the worst," guilty of the polluting acts of patricide and incest with his mother.

As destructive as this worldview is, it provides Oedipus with the only *meaning* structure available to him. Thus, he derives a secondary gain from insisting on his guilt and the impossibility of any redemption. The very sense of being trapped by the maddening labyrinth of Greek society and its inherent fatalism may lead to the extreme of suicide as the only exit from the prison of a cyclical, purposeless life. For life itself is a riddle and a fatalistic trap in this ancient Greek and Roman world. Indeed, it seems as if the Oracle of Delphi (the *Pythia*) uses the unintelligible riddle as her form of communication, giving no usable information.

Let us return to the argument of classicist Bruce Heiden that the Greeks actually preferred communication that had no usable life message. He cites Sophocles fragment 771 in this regard:

> And I thoroughly understand that the god is this way: To the wise, always a poser of riddles in divine speech, but to the foolish a teacher of lessons, trivial and concise.

And his penetrating analysis that "the different addressees for whom Apollo's speeches are either lessons or riddles do not exercise different linguistic competencies but different degrees of wisdom. The acquisition of the positive *meaning* of the teaching surprisingly accords with stupidity, while the riddle, whose characteristic is denial of *meaning*, accords with positive wisdom."[25] This is an extraordinary statement, perhaps underlying much of our educational system. Education is presently taught as a riddle. It does not help people in their actual lives, but only serves to confuse them, and leave them searching fruitlessly and endlessly for *meaning* extrinsic to their own behavior. Let us return to the paradigmatic story of Oedipus and the blind prophet Teiresias to illustrate this point.

Teiresias and Oedipus

Unbeknownst to him, Oedipus has killed his father Laius on the road from Corinth to Thebes, while trying to avoid a prophecy that he is destined to

---

24. Deut 14:1.
25. Heiden, "Eavesdropping on Apollo, "236–37.

kill his father and marry his mother, whom he mistakenly thinks are the king and queen of Corinth. Oedipus subsequently saves travelers to Thebes from being devoured by the riddling Sphinx. Oedipus solves her riddle and she jumps off a rock to her destruction. Oedipus, in turn, is rewarded by being presented the widow of the king of Thebes, Laius, as a wife. He impregnates her and begets four children. Oedipus seems unaware of the identity of his biological parents and has in fact tried his utmost to avoid incest or patricide. Yet he has committed both, and Thebes is now in the throes of a great pestilence. Oedipus believes that this is due to the unsolved murder of Laius and sincerely attempts to find his killer to remove the pestilence from Thebes.

Oedipus summons the blind prophet Teiresias, who knows Oedipus is the cause of the pestilence, to help him. Rather than provide a parable to Oedipus to help make him aware of his actions and accept them, and perhaps find a solution, Teiresias infuriates Oedipus with his evasive, cutting answers. Here are some examples. Teiresias begins his riddling as follows, taunting Oedipus with regard to the total futility of wisdom. "Alas, alas! How dreadful it can be to have wisdom when it brings no benefit to the man possessing it."[26]

Teiresias continues to respond maddingly: "You are all ignorant. I will not reveal the troubling things inside."[27] And when Oedipus, provoked beyond endurance, insults Teiresias regarding his blindness, Teiresias responds as follows with some of the most maddening, vengeful, and chilling lines in all literature. "So I say this to you, since you have chosen to insult my blindness—you have your eyesight, and you do not see how miserable you are, or where you live, or who it is who shares your household . . . Those eyes of yours which now can see so clearly, will be dark. What harbor will not echo with your cries?"[28]

Teireisas taunts Oedipus with one vicious riddle after another, entrapping him more and more in an endless labyrinth. If he has something to say to Oedipus, we must ask why he does not say it straight out, or in parable form, rather than entrap him with maddening riddles that do nothing but lead him to a labyrinth and endless search for *meaning* and to a tragic ending. Oedipus is indeed Camus's Sisyphus.

---

26. Sophocles, *Oedipus the King*, ll. 374–76.
27. Sophocles, *Oedipus the King*, ll. 390–92.
28. Sophocles, *Oedipus the King*, ll. 410–15, 19–20.

Nathan and David

The biblical prophet Nathan, in contrast, uses parables in a *purposive* way to effect genuine repentance and change in King David. David has slept with Bathsheba, the wife of Uriah the Hittite, a member of David's elite corps of warriors. She becomes pregnant by David and tells him so. David then asks that Uriah be sent to him from the battlefield and tries to conceal his adultery with Bathsheba by twice urging Uriah to go home and lie with his wife. Davis thus hopes to deceive Uriah into thinking he is the father of the baby that Bathsheba is carrying. However, Uriah twice refuses to lie with his wife out of loyalty to his men, who are encamped in the open field of battle. "My master's servants are encamped in the open field, and shall I then come to my house to eat and to drink and to lie with my wife?"[29]

David responds by writing a letter to Joab and sends it by the hand of Uriah, saying, "Put Uriah in the face of the fiercest battling and draw back, so that he will be struck down and die."[30] Uriah is killed and Joab reports his death back to David. After Bathsheba hears that her husband has died and grieves, David brings her into his house and marries her. And she bears him a son.[31]

Enter the prophet Nathan, who is sent by the Lord and comes to David with the following parable. Two men lived in the same town; one was rich and the other poor. The rich man had sheep and cattle, in great abundance. And the poor man had nothing save one little ewe that he had bought and whom he had nurtured as a daughter from infancy. A wayfarer came to the rich man, who used his power to take the poor man's ewe and slaughter it for the meal rather than slaughter any of his own many sheep and cattle.

David's anger "flares hot against the man," and he says to Nathan, "As the Lord lives, doomed is the man who has done this, and the poor man's ewe he shall pay back fourfold, in as much as he has done this thing, and because he has no pity!" And in one of the most famous lines in all of literature, Nathan says to David: "You are the man!" Nathan uses this parable to drive home the point that David is the rich man, Uriah is the poor man, and Bathsheba is the ewe that David has taken from Uriah, and has gone even further in arranging for Uriah to be killed. To make it worse, David was aware of all that he had done.

When David is made to confront what he has done, he acknowledges his sin, saying, "I have offended against the Lord." He is not left searching

---

29. 2 Sam 11:11.
30. 2 Sam 11:15.
31. 2 Sam 11:26-27.

endlessly for *meaning* as is Oedipus, but can take *purposive* action. Nathan replies to David that the Lord has remitted his offense and that David shall not die. But the new son born to David and Bathsheba will die, which he does. David grieves and atones in a *purposive manner*, and he and Bathsheba produce another son, Solomon, who will succeed David as king of Israel.[32]

Suppose Oedipus has been able to summon Nathan to unravel the reason for the pestilence in Thebes. Is there a parable he might have told Oedipus to enable him to repent the way David does (given the caveat that the Greek Zeus does not call for repentance or accept it in the same manner as the biblical God)? I have suggested such a riddle in both *Oedipus Redeemed* and *Oedipus the Teacher*, the two successor plays to *Oedipus in Jerusalem*. Here it is:

> There was a man who was told he was going to kill the lamb he had raised from its youth and eat it. To avoid doing this, he gave the lamb to a shepherd to guard it from being slaughtered. But the shepherd suffered financial failures and had to sell the lamb to a butcher. And the first man went to the butcher and bought the lamb and slaughtered it and ate it. without realizing it was his lamb. He had tried to protect his lamb.[33]

This is a parable that could have helped Oedipus accept his actions and begin to deal with the consequences. He would have realized that there was no need for him to feel guilty for what he had done, and indeed been able to accept the reality that he had in fact tried to avoid this but had been entrapped by a set of circumstances he was not aware of. He had been trying to live *purposively* but had been trapped by endless riddles into a self-destructive search for *meaning*.

In my third play in this trilogy, *Oedipus the Teacher*, Oedipus does find a purposive way of living, ending his fruitless search for meaning, and decides to return to Thebes with his surviving daughter, Ismene, to teach the Greeks the lessons he has learned in Jerusalem. He specifically contrasts the destructive riddles endemic in Greek narratives to the parables emerging in biblical text. While the former involves a needless and fruitless search for *meaning* and make genuine growth impossible, the latter allow and even facilitate the living of a life with *purpose*. Living *purposively* represents the essence of a biblical approach to life. *Meaning* does not have to be searched for, and indeed cannot be. Rather, it is a natural byproduct of living a *purposeful*, creative life.

32. 2 Sam 12.

33. Kaplan, *Oedipus Redeemed*, act 2, scene 6, p. 57; *Oedipus the Teacher*, act 2, scene 6, p. 77.

Friedrich Nietzsche puts it this way: "He who has a *why* to live can bear almost any *how*."[34] And this *why* stems from an inner sense of *purpose*. We have argued in this book that this sense of *purpose*, of *purposive* living, must come from within and be syntonic with oneself. In contrast, an endless search for *meaning* is often dystonic with oneself and leads nowhere good (cases in point, Zeno the Stoic and Patient Charlotte).

It is worth repeating Nicholas Wolterstorff's comments with which we began this book.

> The ancient Greek writers had a tragic view of life. Theirs was a culture of honor and shame; they admired the hero. But the hero often found himself enmeshed in a situation where death provided the only alternative to living in shame. The fates had decreed. There was no other way out . . . [However,] the biblical God is not one who decrees our fate but one who has created each of us as a creature of worth, and who loves us . . . In this world, heroism is not called for; it's enough that we be grateful and make good use of the life that's given us.[35]

To summarize this book in one sentence: *Meaning* cannot be found directly, but only as a consequence of living with *purpose*. The biblical Job understood this, but Zeno the Stoic did not.

---

34. Nietzsche, *Twilight of the Idols*, 12.
35. Kaplan and Schwartz, *Psychology of Hope*.

Bibliography

Aeschylus. *Prometheus Bound*. In *The Complete Greek Drama*, edited by Whitney J. Oates and Eugene O'Neill Jr., translated by Paul Elmore More, 1:127–66. New York: Random House, 1938.

———. *The Seven Against Thebes*. In *The Complete Greek Drama*, edited by Whitney J. Oates and Eugene O'Neill Jr., translated by E. D. A. Moreland, 89–126. New York: Random House, 1938.

Alvarez, Al. *The Savage God*. New York: Random House, 1970.

Andersen, Hans Christian. "The Emperor's New Clothes." In *Hans Andersen's Fairy Tales*, edited by H. J. Stickney, 336–44. Chicago: Ginn, 1915.

Apollodorus. *The Library*. Translated by M. Simpson. Amherst: University of Massachusetts Press, 1976.

Babylonia Talmud. Vilna edition. Jerusalem: n.p., 1978.

Baltuck, Naomi. *Apples from Heaven: Multicultural Folk Tales about Stories and Storytellers*. North Haven, CT: Linnet, 1995.

Berman, Saul. "Jewish Environmental Values: The Dynamic Tension between Nature and Human Needs." In *Human Values and the Environment*. IES Report 140. University of Wisconsin, Madison, 1992.

Besser, Anne C., and Kalman J. Kaplan. "The Good Samaritan: Jewish and American Legal Perspectives." *Journal of Law and Religion* 10.1 (1993) 193–219.

Birge, Darice Elizabeth. "Sacred Groves in the Ancient Greek World." PhD diss., University of California, Berkeley, 1982.

Bloom, Alan. *The Closing of the American Mind*. New York: Simon & Schuster, 1987.

Boccaccio, Giovanni. *The Decameron*. Translated by G. H. McWilliam. London: Penguin, 2003.

Boman, Thorlief. *Hebrew Thought Compared with Greek*. Philadelphia: Westminster, 1960.

Browning, Robert. "*Pheidippides*." In *Dramatic Idyls*, 29–44. New York. Horton, 1879.

Buber, Martin. *The Hebrew Humanism of Martin Buber*. Translated by Noah J. Jacobs. Detroit: Wayne State University, 1973.

———. "Plato and Isaiah." In *Israel and the World*, 111–12. New York: Shocken, 1963.

Bugliosi, Vincent N., with Curt Gentry. *Helter Skelter: The True Story of the Manson Murders*. New York: Norton, 1994.
Camus, Albert. *The Myth of Sisyphus*. Translated by Justin O'Brien. New York: Vintage, 1955.
———. *The Plague*. Translated by Stuart Gilbert. New York: Knopf, 1948.
———. *The Rebel: An Essay on Man in Revolt*. Translated by Anthony Bower. New York: Vintage, 1956.
———. *The Stranger*. Translated by Stuart Gilbert. New York: Vintage, 1956.
Cicero. *De Finibus Bonorum et Malorum*. Translated by H. Rackham. New York: Macmillan, 1914.
———. *Tusculan Disputations*. Translated by J. E. King. Loeb Classical Library. Cambridge, MA: Harvard University Press, 1945.
Cohen, S. J. D. "Masada, Literature, Tradition, Archaeological Remains, and the Credibility of Josephus." *Journal of Jewish Studies* 33 (1982) 385-405.
Conon. *Narrationes Quinquaginta et Parthenii Narrationes Amatoriae*. Göttingen: Dietrich, 1798.
Cox, Daniel, and Robert P. Jones. *Changing Religious Identity (Unaffiliated)*. American Values Atlas. Public Religion Research Institute, 2016.
de Tocqueville, Alexis. *Democracy in America*. Translated, edited, and with an introduction by H. G. Mansfield and D. Winthrop. Chicago: University of Chicago Press, 2000.
Defoe, Daniel. *A Journal of the Plague Year*. Boston: D. Estes, 1904.
Diogenes Laertius. *Lives of Eminent Philosophers*. Translated by Robert D. Hicks. Loeb Classical Library. Cambridge: Harvard University Press, 1972.
Dodds, Eric R. "On Misunderstanding the 'Oedipus Rex.'" *Greece and Rome*, 2nd ser., 13.1 (1966) 37-49.
Donne, John. *Biathanatos*. Edited by Ernest W. Sullivan II. Cranbury, NJ: Associated University Press, 1984.
Droge, Arthur. J., and James D. Tabor. *A Noble Death: Suicide and Martyrdom among Christians and Jews in Antiquity*. San Francisco: Harper, 1992.
Durkheim, Emil. *Suicide*. Translated by J. A. Spaulding and G. Simpson. Glencoe, IL: Free Press, 1951.
Erikson, Erik. *Identity, Youth and Crisis*. New York: Norton, 1968.
Euripides. *Alcestis*. Translated by Richard Aldington. In *The Complete Greek Drama*, edited by Whitney J. Oates and Eugene O'Neill Jr., 2:677-722. New York: Random House, 1938.
———. *Andromache*. Translated by E. F. Coleridge. In *The Complete Greek Drama*, edited by Whitney J. Oates and Eugene O'Neill Jr., 1:847-88. New York: Random House, 1938.
———. *The Bacchae*. Translated by G. Murray. In *The Complete Greek Drama*, edited by Whitney J. Oates and Eugene O'Neill Jr., 2:227-28. New York: Random House, 1938.
———. *Hecuba*. Translated by F. M. Stalwall. In *The Complete Greek Drama*, edited by Whitney J. Oates and Eugene O'Neill Jr., 1:807-46. New York: Random House, 1938.
———. *The Heracleidae*. Translated by E. P. Coleridge. In *The Complete Greek Drama*, edited by Whitney J. Oates and Eugene O'Neill Jr., 1:885-918. New York: Random House, 1938.

———. *Hippolytus*. Translated by E. P. Coleridge. In *The Complete Greek Drama*, edited by Whitney J. Oates and Eugene O'Neill Jr., 1:763–806. New York: Random House, 1938.

———. *Iphigenia in Aulis*. Translated by F. M. Stawall. In *The Complete Greek Drama*, edited by Whitney J. Oates and Eugene O'Neill Jr., 2:289–350. New York: Random House, 1938.

———. *The Phoenissae*. Translated by E. P. Coleridge. In *The Complete Greek Drama*, edited by Whitney J. Oates and Eugene O'Neill Jr., 2:171–226. New York: Random House, 1938.

———. *The Suppliants*. Translated by E. P. Coleridge. In *The Complete Greek Drama*, edited by Whitney J. Oates and Eugene O'Neill Jr., 1:919–58. New York: Random House, 1938.

Exline, J. J., et al. "Anger, Exit, and Assertion: Do People See Protest toward God as Morally Acceptable?" *Psychology of Religion and Spirituality* 4.4 (2012) 264–77.

Faber, Milton. *Suicide and Greek Tragedy*. New York: Sphinx, 1970.

Finkelstein, Louis. *Sifre on Deuteronomy*. New York: Jewish Theological Seminary of America; reprint, Berlin: Gesellschaft zur Förderung der Wissenschaft des Judentums, 1969.

Flacelière, Robert. *Daily Life in Greece at the Time of Pericles*. Translated by Peter Green. New York: Macmillan, 1974.

Frankfort, Henri, et al. *Before Philosophy*. Harmondsworth, UK: Penguin, 1964.

Frankl, Viktor E. *Man's Search for Meaning*. Part 1 translated by Ilse Lasch. Boston: Beacon Press, 2006.

Fredericson, Michael, and Anuruddh K. Misra. "Epidemiology and Aetiology of Marathon Running Injuries." *Sports Medicine* 37.4–5 (2007) 437–39.

Freud, Sigmund. *Totem and Taboo*. In *The Standard Edition of the Complete Works of Sigmund Freud*, translated and edited by James Strachey, 13:1–161. London: Hogarth, 1913.

Friedlander, Ludwig. *Roman Life and Manners: Under the Early Empire*. London: Routledge, 1928–36.

Goldberg, Nathan. *Passover Haggadah*. New York, KTAV, 1966.

Goleman, Daniel. "Bruno Bettelheim Dies at 86: Psychoanalyst of Vast Impact." *New York Times*, March 14, 1990.

Gouldner, Alvin. *Enter Plato*. New York: Basic Books, 1965.

Graves, Robert. *The Greek Myths*. Vols. 1–2. London: Pelican, 1960.

Gray, John. *Men Are from Mars, Women Are from Venus*. New York: Thorsons, 1992.

Haberman, Abraham Meir. *Sefer Gezerot Ashkenaz ve-Tsarfat*. Jerusalem: Sifre Tarshish be-siyuʻa Mosad ha-Rav Ḳuḳ, 1946.

Hadda, Janet. *Passionate Women, Passive Men: Suicide in Yiddish Literature*. Albany: State University of New York Press, 2012.

Heiden, Bruce. "Eavesdropping on Apollo: Sophocles' Oedipus the King." *Literary Imagination* 7.2 (2005) 233–57.

Herodotus. *The Histories*. Translated by Aubrey DeSelincourt. Baltimore: Penguin, 1961.

Hesiod. *The Works and Days, Theogony, The Shield of Heracles*. Translated by Richmond Lattimore. Ann Arbor Paperbacks. Ann Arbor: University of Michigan Press, 1991.

Holstein, Martha. "Dying Cardinal Bernardin's Way." *Park Ridge Center Bulletin* 1 (1997).

Homer. *The Iliad*. Translated by A. Lang et al., introduction by Gilbert Highet. New York: Modern Library, 1950.

———. *The Odyssey*. Translated by S. H. Butcher and A. Lang. Introduction by Gilbert Highet. New York: Modern Library, 1950.

Hughes, J. Donald. *Pan's Travail: Environmental Problems in Ancient Greece and Rome.* Baltimore: John Hopkins University Press, 1996.

———. "Sacred Groves: The Gods, Forest Protection, and Sustained Yield in the Ancient World." In *History of Sustained-Yield Forestry: A Symposium*, edited by Harold K. Steen, 331–43. Santa Cruz, CA: Forest History Society, 1984.

Hyginus. *Fabulae*. In *Apollodorus' Library and Hygini' Fabulae: Two Handbooks of Greek Mythology*, translated with introduction by R. Scott Smith and Stephen M. Trzaskoma. Indianapolis: Hackett, 2007.

Jones, Tommie Lee, dir. *The Sunset Limited*. Screenplay by Cormac McCarthy. Produced for television by Home Box Office (HBO), the Javelina Film Company and Professor Productions. HBO, 2011.

Kannicht, R., et al., eds. *Tragocorum, Graecorum, Fragmenta*. Gottingen: Vandenhoeck and Ruprecht, 1971–2004.

Kaplan, Kalman J. "Biblical Humanism and Suicide Prevention: Where Did the Greeks Go Wrong?" In *The Waning of the Spirit: Jubilee Book in Honor of Shlomo Giora Shoham*, edited by C. Ben Noon, 55–78. Tel Aviv: IDRA, 2019.

———. "Hope Unbound: Using Biblical Narratives to Affirm Life and Prevent Suicide." *Military Chaplain* 87.2 (2013) 23–27.

———. "Isaac and Oedipus: A Reexamination of the Father-Son Relationship." *Judaism* 39 (1990) 73–81.

———. "Isaac versus Oedipus: An Alternative View." *Journal of the American Academy of Psychoanalysis* 30.4 (2002) 707–17.

———. "Jonah and Narcissus: Self-Integration versus Self-destruction in Human Development." *Studies in Formative Spirituality* 8 (1987) 33–54.

———. "Jonah versus Narcissus." In *Jewish Approaches to Suicide, Martyrdom and Euthanasia*, edited by Kalman J. Kaplan and Matthew B. Schwartz, 186–96. Northvale, NJ: Aronson, 1998.

———. *Living Biblically: Ten Guides for Fulfillment and Happiness*. Eugene, OR: Wipf & Stock, 2012.

———. "Martha Wichorek's Death." *First Things* 24.6 (2014) 17–19.

———. *Oedipus in Jerusalem: A Play in Two Acts*. Eugene, OR: Wipf & Stock, 2015.

———. *Oedipus Redeemed: Seeing through Listening*. Eugene, OR: Wipf & Stock, 2019.

———. *Oedipus the Teacher: A Return to Thebes*. Eugene, OR: Wipf & Stock, 2019.

———. *Right to Die versus Sacredness of Life*. Amityville, NY: Baywood, 1999–2000.

———. "Shneidman's Definition of Suicide and Jewish Law: A Brief Note." In *Jewish Approaches to Suicide, Martyrdom and Euthanasia*, edited by K. J. Kaplan and Matthew B. Schwartz, 78–79. Northvale, NJ: Aronson, 1998.

———. "Suicide and Suicide Prevention: Greek versus Biblical Perspectives." *Omega* 24 (1991–92) 227–39.

———. "TILT: Teaching Individuals to Live Together." *Transactional Analysis Journal* 18.3 (1988) 220–30.

———. *TILT: Teaching Individuals to Live Together*. Philadelphia: Brunner, 1998.

———. "TILT for Couples: Helping Couples Grow Together." *Transactional Analysis Journal* 20 (1990) 229–41.

———. "Towards a Biblical Psychology: Ten Commandments for Mental Health." *Filsosofia Oggi* 32-N.128-E-14 (October–December 2009) 279–303.

———. "Towards a Biblical Psychology for Modern Israel: Ten Guides for Healthy Living." *Israel Affairs* 22.2 (2016) 291–317. doi:10.1080/13537121.2016.1140349.

Kaplan, Kalman J., and James W. Anderson. "Freud, Greek Narratives, and Biblical Counter-Narratives: A Dialogue." *Clio's Psyche* 20.1 (2013) 101–11.

Kaplan, Kalman J., and Paul Cantz. *Biblical Psychotherapy: Reclaiming Scriptural Narratives for Positive Psychology and Suicide Prevention.* Lanham: Lexington, 2017.

———. "Recovering Biblical Narratives for Positive Psychology and Suicide Prevention in Modern Israel." *Israel Affairs* 24.3 (2018) 395–420. doi: 10.1080/13537121.2018.1454017.

Kaplan. Kalman J., and Mary Leonhardi. "Kevorkian, Martha Wichorek and Us: A Personal Account." In *Right to Die versus Sacredness of Life*, edited by Kalman J. Kaplan, 67–70. Amityville, NY: Baywood, 2000.

Kaplan, Kalman. J., and Moriah Markus-Kaplan. "Covenant versus Contract as Two Modes of Relationship-Orientation: On Reconciling Possibility and Necessity." *Journal of Psychology and Judaism* 4 (1979) 100–116.

Kaplan, Kalman J., and. Nancy A. O'Connor. "From Mistrust to Trust: Through a Stage Vertically." In *The Course of Life*, edited by S. I. Greenspan and G. H. Pollock, 6:153–98. New York: International Universities Press, 1993.

Kaplan, Kalman J., and Lisa T. Ross. "Life Ownership Orientation and Attitudes toward Abortion, Suicide and Capital Punishment." *Journal of Psychology and Judaism* 19.1 (1995) 177–93.

Kaplan, Kalman J., and Matthew B. Schwartz., eds. *Jewish Approaches to Suicide, Martyrdom and Euthanasia.* Northvale, NJ: Aronson, 1998.

———. *Parables and Riddles in Ancient and Modern Teaching: Achilles, a Hare and Two Tortoises.* Newcastle upon Tyne: Cambridge, 2019.

———. *A Psychology of Hope: A Biblical Response to Tragedy and Suicide.* Grand Rapids: Eerdmans, 2008.

———. *The Seven Habits of the Good Life: How the Biblical Virtues Free Us from the Seven Deadly Sins.* Lanham, MD: Rowman & Littlefield, 2008.

Kaplan, Kalman J., and Shirley Worth. "Individuation-Attachment and Suicide Trajectory: A Developmental Guide for the Clinician." *Omega: Journal of Death and Dying* 27 (1993) 297–37.

Kaplan, Kalman J., et al. "A Biblical View of Eating and Nutrition: Restraint, Respect, Purpose and Order." Delivered at the Third Annual Conference on Medicine and Religion, Chicago, March 7–9, 2014.

———. "A Biblical View of Health, Sickness and Healing: Overcoming the Traditional Greek View of Medicine." In *The Healing Power of Spirituality, How Religion Helps Humans Thrive*, edited by J. H. Ellens, 3: 230–42, Westport, CT: Praeger, 2010.

———. *Family: Biblical and Psychological Foundations.* New York: Human Sciences, 1984.

———. "Why Does Zeno the Stoic Hold His Breath?: Zenoism as a New Variable for Studying Suicide." *Omega: The Journal of Death and Dying* 56.4 (2008) 369–400.

———. "Zenoism, Depression and Attitudes toward Suicide and Physician-Assisted Suicide: The Moderating Effects of Religiosity and Gender." *Ethics and Medicine* 24.3 (2008) 167–87.

Karo, Joseph. *Shulchan Aruch.* Venice, 1565.

Kelman, Herbert C., and V. Lee Hamilton. *Crimes of Obedience: Toward a Social Psychology of Authority and Responsibility*. New Haven, CT: Yale University Press, 1989.
Koch, Horst J. "Suicides and Suicide Ideation in the Bible: An Empirical Survey." *Act a Psychiatrica Scandinavica* 112.3 (2005) 167–72.
Larcher, Pierre Henri. *Larcher's Notes on Herodotus: Historical and Critical Comments on the History of Herodotus*. From the French. Edited by William Cooley Desborough. London: Whitaker, 1844.
Lerner, Melvin J., and Dale T. Miller. "Just World Hypothesis and the Attribution Process: Looking Forward and Ahead." *Psychological Bulletin* 85.5 (1978) 1030–51.
Liddell, Henry G., Robert Scott, and Henry Stuart Jones. *A Greek-English Lexicon*. 9th ed. Oxford: Clarendon, 1996.
Lifton, Robert J. *The Nazi Doctors: A Study of the Psychology of Evil*. London: Macmillan, 1986.
Longfellow, Henry W., and C. H. Bing. *The Midnight Ride of Paul Revere*. Brooklyn: Handprint B., 2001.
Macera, Caroline A., et al. "Postrace Morbidity among Runners." *American Journal of Preventive Medicine* 7.4 (1991) 194–98.
Maimonides, Moses. *The Book of Divine Commandments* (*Sefer Ha Mitzvot*). London: Soncino, 1940.
———. *Mishne, Torah: A Collection of Manuscripts from the Library of the Jewish Theological Seminary*. Ann Arbor, MI: University Microfilms International, 1980.
Mann, Thomas. *Death in Venice*. Translated with Commentary by Stanley Appelbaum. Mineola, NY: Dover, 1995.
Markus-Kaplan, Moriah, and Kalman J. Kaplan. "The Typology, Diagnosis, Pathologies and Treatment-intervention of Hellenic versus Hebraic Personality Styles: A Proposal on the Psychology of Interpersonal Distancing." *Journal of Psychology and Judaism* 3 (1979) 153–67.
Marquez, Gabriel Garcia. *Love in the Time of Cholera*. Translated by Edith Grossman. New York: Knopf, 1988.
Marti, Bernard, et al. "On the Epidemiology of Running Injuries: The 1984 Bern Grand-Prix Study." *American Journal of Sports Medicine* 16.3 (1988) 285–94.
Marshall, Alfred, ed. *NASB Interlinear Greek-English New Testament*. Grand Rapids: Zondervan, 1984.
May, Rollo. *Existential Psychology*. New York: Random House, 1961.
Milgram, Stanley. *Obedience to Authority: An Experimental View*. New York: Harper and Row, 1974.
Midrash Rabbah. Vols. 1–10. Edited by. H. Freedman and Maurice Simon. Translated by J. Israelstam and Judah Slotkin. London: Soncino, 1939.
Midrash Rabbah, with Commentaries of Mattenot Kehuna, Rashi, Messoret Hamidrash, Yefeh To'ar, Perush HaMeharzo. 2 vols. Reprint, New York: Grossman, 1953.
Mitchell, C. Ben. "Of Euphemisms and Euthanasia: The Language Games of the Nazi Doctors and Some Implications for the Modern Euthanasia Movement." *Omega* 40.1 (1999–2000) 255–65.
Nathan, J. "Injury Prevention in Marathon Runners." *Journal of Outdoor Activities* 7.1 (2013) 32–39.
New English Bible with Apocrypha. Oxford: Oxford University Press, 1970.
Nietzsche, Friedrich Wilhelm. *Twilight of the Idols, The Anti-Christ*. Translated by R. J. Hollingdale. London: Penguin, 1990.

Oldstone, Michael B. A. *Viruses, Plagues & History*. New York: Oxford University Press, 1998.
Ovid. *Fasti*. Translated and edited by Anthony J. Boyle and Roger D. Woodward. London: Penguin, 2000.
———. *Metamorphoses*. Translated by Charles Boer. Dallas: Spring, 1989.
Oxford Classical Dictionary. Edited by N. G. L. Hammond and H. H. Scullard. 2nd ed. Oxford: Clarendon, 1970.
Pepys, Samuel. *Diary of Samuel Pepys*. New York: Macmillan, 1905.
Petronius Arbiter. *The Satyricon*. Translated by William Arrowsmith. Ann Arbor: University of Michigan Press, 1959.
Plato. *Critias*. Translated by A. E. Taylor. In *Plato: The Collected Dialogues, Including the Letters*, edited by Edith Hamilton and Huntington Cairns, 1212–24. Bollingen Series 71. Princeton, NJ: Princeton University Press, 1999.
———. *Republic*. Translated by P. Shorrey. In *Plato: The Collected Dialogues, Including the Letters*, edited by Edith Hamilton and Huntington Cairns, 575–844. Bollingen Series 71. Princeton, NJ: Princeton University Press, 1999.
Plutarch. *Morals: Theosophical Essays*. Translated by W. C. King. London: Bell, 1898.
Poe, Edgar Allan. *The Mask of the Red Death: A Fantasy*. Philadelphia: Graham's Magazine, 1842.
Pullman, Philip. *Fairy Tales from the Brothers Grimm: A New English Version*. New York: Penguin, 2013.
Rashi. New York: Pardes, 1962.
Rosenblum, Jordan. Food and Identity in Early Rabbinic Judaism. New York: Cambridge University Press, 2010.
Saragiotto, Bruno T., et al. "What Are the Main Risk Factors for Running-related Injuries?" *Sports Medicine* 44.8 (2014) 1153–63.
Schwartz, Matthew B. and Kalman J. Kaplan. *Biblical Stories for Psychotherapy and Counseling: A Sourcebook*. Binghamton, NY: Haworth Pastoral, 2004.
———. "War, Peace and the Military in Biblical and Ancient Greek Societies." In *Routledge International Handbook of Military Psychology and Mental Health*, edited by Updesh Kumar, 13–37. London: Taylor & Francis, 2019.
Sefer Hachinuch. Jerusalem: Machon Yerushalayim, 1988.
Seneca the Elder. *Oratorum et rhetorum sententiae divisiones, colores*. Translated by M. Winterbottom. Cambridge, MA: Harvard University Press, 1974.
Seneca the Younger. *Seneca*. Cambridge, MA: Harvard University Press, 1979.
Seneca Lucius Annaeus. *De Ira (Anger, Mercy, Revenge)*. Translated by Robert A. Kaster and Martha C. Nussbaum. Chicago: University of Chicago Press, 2010.
Shachar, Giora Y. "Unpublished Lectures on Medical Principles of Maimonides." Israel, 2013.
Shakespeare, William. *Titus Andronicus*. In *The Complete Works of William Shakespeare*, introduction by Michael A. Kramer, 151–80. San Diego: Canterbury Classics, 2014.
Shemesh, Yael. "Suicide in the Bible." *Jewish Bible Quarterly* 37.3 (2009) 157.
Shestov, Lev. *Athens and Jerusalem*. Translated by B. Martin. New York: Simon & Schuster, 1966.
Shochet, Elijah J. *Animal Life in Jewish Tradition*. New York: Ktav, 1984.
Shoham, Shlomo G. *Genesis of Genesis: The Mytho-Empiricism of Creation*. Newcastle upon Tyne: Cambridge Scholars, 2011.
———. *The Myth of Tantalus*. St. Lucia: University of Queensland Press, 1979.

Silove, D., et al. "No Refuge from Terror: The Impact of Detention on the Mental Health of Trauma-Affected Refugees Seeking Asylum in Australia." *Transcultural Psychiatry* 44.3 (2007) 359–93.
Simon, Bennett. *Mind and Madness in Ancient Greece: The Classical Roots of Modern Psychiatry.* Ithaca, NY: Cornell University Press, 1978.
Slater, Philip E. *The Glory of Hera: Greek Mythology and the Greek Family.* Boston: Beacon, 1968.
Snell, Bruno. *The Discovery of the Mind: The Greek Origins of European Thought.* New York: Dover, 1953.
Snell, Bruno, and Richard Kannicht, eds. *Tragocorum Graecorum Fragmenta.* Vol. 1. Gottingen: Vandenhoeck & Ruprecht, 1986.
Soloveitchik, Joseph B. *Halakhic Man.* Translated by L. Kaplan. Philadephia: Jewish Publication Society of America, 1983.
———. "The Lonely Man of Faith." *Tradition* 7.2 (1965) 10–16.
Sophocles. *Ajax.* In *The Complete Greek Drama: Volume I,* edited by Whitney J. Oates and Eugene O'Neill Jr. and translated by R. C. Trevelyan, 315–68. New York: Random House, 1938.
———. *Antigone.* Translated by R. C. Jebb. In *The Complete Greek Drama,* edited by Whitney J. Oates and Eugene O'Neill Jr., 1:423–60. New York: Random House, 1938.
———. *Oedipus at Colonus.* Translated by R. C. Jebb. In *The Complete Greek Drama,* edited by Whitney J. Oates and Eugene O'Neill Jr., 1:613–70. New York: Random House, 1938.
———. *Oedipus the King.* Translated by R. C. Jebb. In *The Complete Greek Drama,* edited by Whitney J. Oates and Eugene O'Neill Jr., 1:369–422. New York: Random House, 1938.
———. *The Trachiniae.* Translated by R. C. Jebb. In *The Complete Greek Drama,* edited by Whitney J. Oates and Eugene O'Neill Jr., 1:465–504. New York: Random House, 1938.
Steinschneider, Moritz. *Alpha Betha de-Ben Sira.* Berlin: n.p., 1858.
Strabo. *Geographica.* Translated by H. C. Hamilton and W. Falconer. New York: Bell, 1854–57.
Tzetzes, Johannes. *Chiliades.* Edited by Gottlieb Kiessling. Hildesheim: Olms, 1963.
Warren, Kay. *Choose Joy: Because Happiness Isn't Enough.* Grand Rapids: Revel, 2012.
Warren, Rick. *The Purpose Driven Life: What on Earth Am I Here For?* Grand Rapids: Zondervan, 2002.
Wellisch, Erich. *Isaac and Oedipus: Studies in Biblical Psychology of the Sacrifice of Isaac.* London: Routledge & Kegan Paul, 1954.
Wu, Andrew, et al. "Religion and Completed Suicide: A Meta-Analysis." *PloS One* 10.6 (2015). doi: 10.1371journal.pone.0131715.
Yerushalmi, Yosef H. *Freud's Moses: Judaism Terminable and Interminable.* New Haven, CT: Yale University Press, 1991.
Ziffer, E. *All the People of the Bible.* Tel Aviv: Havav, 2006.
———. *The Stoics, Epicureans, and Sceptics.* Translated by O. J. Reichel. New York: Russell & Russell, 1962.
Zubin, Joseph, and Bonnie Spring. "Vulnerability—A New View of Schizophrenia." *Journal of Abnormal Psychology* 86.2 (1977) 103–26.

Index

Note: n indicates footnotes, and italicized page numbers indicate illustrations.

Aaron [biblical character], 96
Aaron the Moor, 90 n. 47
Abel, 110
Abimelech, 35–36
Abraham, 19, 25, 104–6, 110
Abram. *See* Abraham
Absalom, 36
Achaeans, 116
Acheron, 30
Achilles, 31–32, 76, 79, 116–17, 124 n. 17
Acts, Book of, 43
Adam, 94, 100, 103, 110
Admetus, King, 32
Aerope, 90 n. 46
Aeschylus, 16, 28, 33–34 nn. 20–21, 38 n. 38, 72
Agamemnon, 33, 79–80, 107, 124 n. 17
Agave, 90 n. 44
Ahitophel, 35–36
Aiolos, 120
Ajax (Sophocles), 29, 31
Ajax [character], 29, 31, 33–34, 37, 79–80, 124 n. 17
Akedah (binding of Isaac), 105–6
Akiba, R., 44 n. 72, 75–76
Alcestis (Euripides), 29, 31–32
Alcestis [character], 29, 32

Algina, 120
altruistic suicide, 29, 33, 35, 37, 43, 76
Alzheimer's disease, 60, 63–65
American Revolution, 7
Andersen, Hans Christian, 21
Andromache (Euripides), 29
anomic suicide, 29–30
Antigone (Sophocles), 29–30, 74
Antigone [character], 29–30, 123
Antiochus Eupator, King, 43
Antiphates, King, 89
Aphrodite, 31
Apollo, 18, 32, 119 n. 1, 127
Argives, the, 32, 75
Argos, Greece, 32, 75
Artemis, 83
Aruch HaShulchan, 35
Asia Minor, 82
Asopos, 120
assassination. *See* death
assisted suicide, 36, 59–62, 64–68
Athena, 31, 73, 79–80
Athens, Greece, 6, 31–32, 46, 75
Athens and Jerusalem (Shestov), 4
Athos Peninsula, 83
Atlas, 120
Atreus, 90 nn. 46–47
Attica, 83

INDEX

Auschwitz, 76 n. 12
Avodah Zarah [Talmudic tractate], 44 n. 72

Baba Batra [Talmudic tractate], 44 n. 72
Baba Kamma [Talmudic tractate], 35 n. 24, 86
Babylonian Talmud, 74
Bacchae (Euripides), 90 n. 44
Baltuck, Naomi, 19
Bathsheba, 129–30
Battle of Marathon, 6
Battles of Lexington and Concord, 7
Bavaria, 45 n. 72
Beatles, the, 2
Beethoven, Ludwig van, 45 n. 72
Bellerophontes, 120
Berachot [Talmudic tractate], 44 n. 72
Berman, R. Saul, 86
Bernardin, Joseph Cardinal, 77
Beruria, 44 n. 72
Besser, Anne, 115
Bethlehem, 107–8
Bettelheim, Bruno, 47
Biathanatos (Donne), 28
Bible
    approach of the
        in clinical cases, 59, 66, 72–73, 77
    life as inherently meaningful as, 4, 11, 13, 17–18, 25, 27, 35–37, 41, 43, 47–48, 56–57, 66, 72–73, 75, 77–78, 81–82, 84, 99, 102–4, 106, 108, 111, 115, 117–21, 123–24, 126–27, 130–31
    life of purpose as, 3–4, 7, 11, 13–14, 17–19, 25–28, 37, 43, 47–51, 56–57, 59, 66, 72–73, 75, 77–79, 81–82, 84–85, 87, 92–93, 95, 97, 99–100, 102–4, 106, 108, 110–11, 113–21, 124–27, 129–31
    role of hope in, 43, 73–75, 102, 106

    suicide prevention as, 4, 38–45, 48, 50, 62, 65–67, 71–72, 77–80
    creation narrative, 4, 13–14, 16–17, 25–27, 42, 56, 81–82, 84–86, 95, 101 n. 88, 103
    Elijah as example of suicide prevention in the, 38–39, 43, 78–80
    God of the, 3–4, 13–14, 16–17, 25–27, 34, 35 n. 24, 36–37, 41, 47–48, 56–57, 66, 74, 76–82, 84–86, 92–96, 100–101, 103, 105–7, 110–11, 113–18, 120–24, 126, 129–31
    Israelites' acceptance of the, 3–4, 11, 37, 74, 95 n. 73, 102, 105–6, 111, 118, 126
    Job as example of suicide prevention in the, 38, 41–42, 48, 50, 62, 65–67, 71–72, 77
    Job's life as purposeful, 48–51, 62, 67, 71–73, 77, 131
    meaning vs. purpose
        in eating, 87, 92–97
        in the environment, 81–82, 84–86
        in fathers and sons, 104–6
        in Greek vs. biblical prophecies, 119–31
        in history, 7, 11
        in illness, 97–99
        in literature, 3–4
        in men and women, 102–3
        in mothers and daughters, 106–8
        in obedience vs. disobedience to authority, 99–102
        in the self and other, 113–15
        in siblings, 108, 110–11
        in Stoic vs. biblical thought, 52–58
        in war and peace, 115–18
    parable as purpose in the, 18–19, 25, 27, 126, 129–30
    suicides in the, 34–38, 43–44
    syllogisms, 124–26
    view of death in the, 4, 11, 26, 28, 34–45, 47–51, 56–59, 65–67,

71–73, 75–78, 80, 98, 107, 110, 113–15, 121–23, 129–31
Bildad, 49
Bnei B'rak, Israel, 44 n. 72
Boaz, 108
Bocaccio, Giovanni, xiii
Boman, Thorlief, 126
Boston, Massachusetts, 7, 11
British Regulars, 10
Brothers Grimm, 19
Browning, Robert, 6, 11
Bugliosi, Vincent, 2 n. 5

Cadmus, 90 n. 44
Cain, 110
California, 3
Camus, Albert, 1–3, 56, 58, 99, 120–21, 123, 128
Canaan, 93, 105
Cantz, Paul, 4, 30, 59, 97
cases, clinical, 59–73, 77, 98 n. 81, 131
Cassandra, 119
Cato, 54
Ceres, 88
Chanukah, 77
chaos, 1, 15–16, 25, 27, 81–82, 92, 124
Charlestown, Massachusetts, 8
Chicago, Illinois, 77
Chimaira, 120
Choose Joy, Because Happiness Is Not Enough (Warren), 3
Christianity, 2, 7, 43, 56, 101 n. 88
Christmas, 77
Chronicles 1, Book of, 35
Chronos, 109
Cicero, 53–55, 72
Circe, 88
Cleanthes, 47, 53
clinical cases, 59–73, 77, 98 n. 81, 131
Clytemnestra, 106–7
Cnidus, 82
Concord, Massachusetts, 10
Conon, General, 48, 56, 113
Continental Army, 11 n. 25
Corinth, Greece, 104, 120, 127–28
covenantal suicide, 37
creation, views of

biblical, 4, 13–14, 16–17, 25–27, 42, 56, 81–82, 84–86, 95, 101 n. 88, 103
Greek, 13–16, 81–84, 86, 101 n. 88
Creon, 30
Cronus, 15, 73, 104, 109
cycle vs. development
in clinical cases, 60
in Greek vs. biblical approaches
to fathers and sons, 105
to life and death, 33, 43
to men and women, 103
to prophecy, 120–27
and the importance of hope, 73
in parables vs. riddles, 25–27
Cyclops/Cyclopes, 15, 89

Dagon, Temple of, 37
daughters and mothers, meaning vs. purpose in
biblical narrative, 106–8
Clytemnestra-Electra, 106–8
Greek narrative, 106–8
Naomi-Ruth, 106–8
David, King, 36, 38, 42, 85, 108, 116–17, 129–30
de Tocqueville, Alexis, 3
death. *see also* suicide
biblical view of, 4, 11, 26, 28, 34–45, 47–51, 56–59, 65–67, 71–73, 75–78, 80, 98, 107, 110, 113–15, 121–23, 129–31
clinical cases of suicide, 59–72, 77, 98 n. 81
God as giving man a choice between life and, 34, 35 n. 24, 36–42, 44 n. 72
in Greek literature, 4, 6, 11, 15, 28–33, 34 n. 21, 35, 38 n. 38, 44, 52–53, 55, 72, 75–76, 79–80, 90 n. 45, 104–5, 107, 110, 112–13, 115, 120, 124 n. 17, 127–28, 131
Greek vs. biblical approaches to life vs., 4–12, 28–45, 47–51, 59, 66, 72–73, 75–77
in history, 2–3, 6–7, 11

death (continued)
  inevitability of, 1, 55–56, 58
  in modern literature, 1–3, 56, 58, 120–21, 123, 128
  in riddles vs. parables, 20, 26, 104–5, 127–30
  Stoic view of, 48, 52–56, 68, 72, 77–78
  while searching for meaning, 1–4, 11–12, 15, 20, 28–37, 46–51, 55–56, 58, 61–62, 65–68, 72, 75–78, 105, 107, 112, 115, 120–21, 127–28, 130–31
  Zeno's view of, 29, 46–53, 55–56, 61–62, 67–68, 72, 75–77
Deianeira, 29–31
Demeter, 88
Democracy in America (de Tocqueville), 3
Demophon, 32, 75
Demosthenes, 29
Depression, Great, 68
Detroit, Michigan, 60, 62, 64
Detroit Free Press, 59
Deucalion, 100–101
Deuteronomy, Book of, 86
development vs. cycle
  in clinical cases, 60
  in Greek vs. biblical approaches
    to fathers and sons, 105
    to life and death, 33, 43
    to men and women, 103
    to prophecy, 120–27
  and the importance of hope, 73
  in parables vs. riddles, 25–27
Diana, 83
Diogenes Laertius, 28, 46–47
disobedience vs. obedience to an authority, meaning vs. purpose in
  biblical narrative, 99–101
  God-Noah, 100–101
  Greek narrative, 99–101
  Zeus-Prometheus, 100–101
Dodds, E. R., 25
Donne, John, 28
Droge, Arthur J., 56, 62
Dubno, Preacher of, 19

Durkheim, Emil, 29, 45 n. 72

Earth, 15–17, 109
eating, meaning vs. purpose in
  biblical narrative, 87, 92–97
  Greek narrative, 87–90, 92–94
  Passover Seder, 92–97
  Roman narrative, 87, 90 n. 47, 91–92
  Trimalchio's dinner, 91–92, 95
Ecclesiastes, Book of, 57, 120–23
Ecclesiastes Rabbah, 44 n. 72
Echo, 112
egoistic suicide, 29–31, 33, 35–37
Egypt, 96, 106, 111, 125
Elah, King, 36
Eleazar, 43
Electra, 106–8
Elijah
  cup of, 96
  suicide prevention of, 38–39, 43, 78–80
  vs. Ajax, 79–80
Eliphaz, 49
Elisha, 80
"The Emperor's New Clothes," 19, 21–25
Encolpius, 92
Endor, Witch of, 38
England, 7–8, 45 n. 72
environment, meaning vs. purpose in the
  biblical creation narrative, 81–82, 84–86
  Greek creation narrative, 81–84, 86
  Roman view, 82–84
Ephraim, 106, 111
Ephyra. *See* Corinth, Greece
Epimetheus, 73, 100, 102
Erysichthon, 88
Esau, 40, 93, 110–11
Eteocles, 33–34 nn. 20–21, 109
Euripides, 28–29, 31–33, 34 n. 21, 38 n. 38, 75–76, 90 n. 44
Europe, 3, 45 n. 72
Eurydice, 29–30
Eurymede, 120
Eurystheus, King, 32, 75

euthanasia. *See* assisted suicide
Evadne, 29
Eve, 102–3, 110
ever min ha'hai (eating living animals), 94
Exodus, Book of, 14, 57, 96
ezer kenegdo (helpmeet opposite), 102–3

Faber, Milton, 28–30
fate (*moira*), 55, 79, 112, 121, 123, 126, 131
Fates, the, 4, 16, 32–33, 131
fathers and sons, meaning vs. purpose in
    Abraham-Isaac, 104–6
    biblical narrative, 104–6
    Greek narrative, 104–5
    Laius-Oedipus, 104–5
Feiger, Geoffrey, 63
Fertile Crescent, 100
fire, Greek vs. biblical approach to man's acquisition of, 73, 86, 94, 99–100, 102
Flood, Greek vs. biblical approach to the Great, 74, 99–102, 121
Fortunata, 92
France, 2–3, 45 n. 72
Franco, Francisco, 45 n. 72
Frankl, Viktor, 2–3, 76 n. 12
Fredericson, Michael, 5, 7
Freud, Sigmund, 45 n. 72, 126
Friedlander, Ludwig, 84
Furies, 16

Gaia, 15, 82–83, 109
Galen, 97
Garden of Eden, 16, 84
Gemara. See Talmud
Genesis, Book of
    parables in the, 25–26
    purposeful nature of life in the, 25, 27, 56, 94, 103, 108, 111
    suicide preventions in the, 38
    views of creation in the, 27, 56, 103
Genesis Rabbah, 44 n. 72
Germany, 2, 99

Gilboa, Mount, 37
Gittin [Talmudic tractate], 44 n. 72
Glaucos, 120
The Glory of Hera: Greek Mythology and the Greek Family (Slater), 6, 13
God
    of the Bible, 3–4, 13–14, 16–17, 25–27, 34, 35 n. 24, 36–37, 41, 47–48, 56–57, 66, 74, 76–82, 84–86, 92–96, 100–101, 103, 105–7, 110–11, 113–18, 120–24, 126, 129–31
    covenant between the Israelites and, 3–4, 11, 37, 74, 95 n. 73, 102, 105–6, 111, 118, 126
    as creator of man and his purpose, 4, 13–14, 16–17, 25–27, 37, 47–51, 56–57, 77–78, 81–82, 84–86, 92–96, 98–101, 103, 105–7, 110–11, 113–18, 120–21, 124, 126, 129–31
    as giver of hope, 74
    giving man a choice between life and death, 34, 35 n. 24, 36–42, 44 n. 72
    meaning vs. purpose in obedience vs. disobedience to an authority, 100–101
    as sole giver and remover of life, 47–51, 60, 66, 76–78, 80, 98–99, 105–6, 122–23
Goliath, 116–17
Good Samaritan statutes, 115
Gornos of Lydda, 44 n. 72
Goths, 90 n. 47
Greece and Greek culture
    creation narrative, 13–16, 81–84, 86, 101 n. 88
    death in literature of, 1, 4, 6, 11, 15, 28–35, 37, 38 n. 38, 44, 46–48, 50, 52–56, 61–62, 67–69, 72, 75–76, 79–80, 90 n. 45, 104–5, 107, 109–10, 112–15, 120–23, 124 n. 17, 127–28, 131
    lack of hope in, 33, 53, 72–76, 102, 126
    lack of suicide prevention in, 34, 55

Greece and Greek culture (continued)
  meaning vs. purpose
    in eating, 87–90, 92–94
    in the environment, 81–84, 86
    in fathers and sons, 104–5
    in history, 7, 11
    in illness, 97–98
    in literature, 1, 4
    in men and women, 102–3
    in mothers and daughters, 106–8
    in obedience vs. disobedience to authority, 99–101
    in prophecy, 119–21, 126–28, 130–31
    in the self and other, 112–15
    in siblings, 108–11
    in war and peace, 115–18
  origin of marathons, 4–7, 11, 72
  search for meaning
    in creation story, 13, 15
    as hopeless, 33, 72–73, 75–76
    in riddles, 18–19, 24–25, 27, 104–5, 126–28, 130
    in Stoic thought, 55, 57, 68
    in suicide, 1, 28–35, 47–48, 50, 55–56, 61–62, 67–68, 72, 76, 112, 115, 120–21, 127
  syllogisms, 124–26

Habinnas, 92
Hadda, Janet, 45 n. 72
Hades, 15, 88, 120
Haemon, 29–30
Hagar, 105, 110
Haggadah, 95
Hama, R., 110
Hanina ben Teradion, R., 44 n. 72
Hannah, 44 n. 72
Haran, 93
Hasmoneans, the, 44 n. 72
HBO, 78
Hebrews. *See* Israelites
Hector, 116
Hecuba (Euripides), 29, 31–32, 76
Hecuba, Queen, 32, 76, 119
Heiden, Bruce, 18, 127
Helen, 116

Hellas, 124
Hellespont, 83
Helter Skelter, 2, 82
Helter Skelter: The True Story of the Manson Murders (Bugliosi), 2 n. 5
Hera, 109
The Heracleidae (Euripides), 29, 31–32
Heracles, 29–32, 75, 109
Hermione, 29
Herod, 44 n. 72
Herodotus, 115
Hesiod, 14–15, 25, 73, 81
Hippocrates, 98
Hippocratic Oath, 97–98
Hippolytus (Euripides), 29, 31
Hippolytus [character], 31–32
Hittites, the, 40, 129
Hobson, 126
Holocaust, 45 n. 72
Homer, 87, 116
hope
  as biblical approach, 43, 73–75, 102, 106
  God as giver of, 74
  Greeks' lack of, 33, 53, 72–76, 102, 126
  importance of, 72–80
  Noah (rainbow), 74, 101–2
  Pandora (urn), 73–74, 102
Horeb, Mount, 39, 80
Hughes, J. Donald, 82–84
Hullin [Talmudic tractate], 44 n. 72
Hyllus, 31

Ice Age, 100
Iliad (Homer), 91, 115–17
Illinois, 77
illness, meaning vs. purpose in
  biblical narrative, 97–99
  Greek narrative, 97–98
  Hippocratic Oath, 97–98
  prayer of Maimonides, 97–99
infanticide. *See* death
intervention, Job, 59, 62–67, 70–71
Iolaus, 32
Iole, 30–31
Iphicles, 109

Iphigenia, 29, 33–34, 75–76
Iphigenia in Aulis (Euripides), 29, 31, 33
Isaac, 40, 104–6, 110–11
Isaac ben Solomon Israeli (I. Judaeus), 97
Ishmael, 105, 110
Ismene, 130
Israel (Jacob). *See* Jacob
Israel, Land of, 36, 44 n. 72, 84, 96, 124, 126, 130
Israelites
   covenant between God and the, 3–4, 11, 37, 74, 95 n. 73, 102, 105–6, 111, 118, 126
   slavery and exodus of the, 96–97, 125
   suicide preventions among the, 40, 113–14
   suicides among the, 36–37, 41
   vs. Goliath, 117
Ithaca, 89
Itys, 90 n. 45

Jabok, River, 93
Jackson, Samuel L., 78–80
Jacob, 40, 93, 106, 108, 110–11
Jakum of Tzeroth, 44 n. 72
Jerusalem, Israel, 96, 126, 130
Jesse, 108
Jesus Christ, 42, 101 n. 88
Jezebel, Queen, 38, 80
Joab, 129
Job
   intervention, 59, 62–67, 70–71
   life of as purposeful, 48–51, 62, 67, 71–73, 77, 131
   suicide prevention of, 38, 41–42, 48–50, 62, 65–67, 71–72, 77
   vs. Zeno, 41–42, 46–52, 72, 77, 131
Job, Book of, 38, 41–42, 49
Jocasta, 25, 29–30, 33 n. 20, 104–5, 109
Jonah
   biblical approach of
      to life and death, 40
      to prophecy, 124
      to the self and other, 113–15
   suicide prevention of, 38–40, 113–15

   vs. Narcissus, 114–15, 124
Jonah, Book of, 38, 119, 124
Jones, Tommy Lee, 78–80
Jordan River, 93
Joseph, 106, 110–11
Joseph Meshitha, R., 44 n. 72
Josephus, Flavius, 43
Jotapata [historical], 43
Judaeus, I. (Isaac ben Solomon Israeli), 97
Judah [biblical], 107
Judaism
   importance of hope in, 76
   meaning vs. purpose in, 11, 56, 86–87, 97–98, 100, 115, 127
   suicides in history of, 43–44, 45 n. 72
Judas Iscariot, 43
Judeans, the, 43
Judges, Book of, 35

Kevorkian, Jack, 59, 62–64
Kings 1, Book of, 35, 38
Koch, Horst J., 43
Koheleth. *See* Ecclesiastes, Book of

Laban, 40, 93
LaBianca, Leno, 2
LaBianca, Rosemary, 2
Laenas, 91
Laestrogons, 89
Laius, King, 104–5, 127–28
Lamentations Rabbah, 44 n. 72
Lamus, 89
Leviticus, Book of, 94–95
Lexington, Massachusetts, 10
Liddell, Henry G., 15, 82
Lirope, 112
The Lives of Eminent Philosophers (Laertius), 46
lo taschit (do not destroy), 16, 84–86, 118
London, England, 45 n. 72
London Marathon, 5
Longfellow, Henry Wadsworth, 7

Macaria, 29, 32–34, 75–76
Maccabees 1, Book of, 43
Maccabees 2, Book of, 43

INDEX

Macera, Caroline A., 5
Machpelah, Cave of, 110
Madrid, Spain, 45 n. 72
Maenads, the, 90
Maimonides, Moses, 95, 97–99
Manasseh, 106, 111
Mann, Thomas, xiii
Man's Search for Meaning (Frankl), 2, 76 n. 12
Manson, Charles and family, 2–3, 82
Marathon, Greece, 5–6
marathons, meaning vs. purpose of running, 4–7, 11, 72
Marc Antony, 29
Marquez, Gabriel Garcia, xiii
Mars, 101
Marti, Bernard, 5
Masada, 43
Massachusetts, 7–8, 10–11
Matthew, Book of, 42–43
May, Rollo, 2
McCarthy, Cormac, 78
meaning
    biblical view of life as inherently full of, 4, 11, 13, 17–18, 25, 27, 35–37, 41, 43, 47–48, 56–57, 66, 72–73, 75, 77–78, 81–82, 84, 99, 102–4, 106, 108, 111, 115, 117–21, 123–24, 126–27, 130–31
    as consequence of purpose, 4, 131
    of Paul Revere's ride, 7–12
    of Pheidippides' run, 4–7, 11, 72
    searching for
        in creation story, 13, 15
        destructiveness of, 2–4, 7, 12, 16–17, 20, 31, 33 n. 20, 34, 48, 50, 56–57, 61–62, 73, 78, 85, 90 n. 44, 101 n. 88, 107, 127, 130
        dying while, 1–4, 11–12, 15, 20, 28–37, 41–43, 46–51, 55–56, 58, 61–62, 65–68, 71–72, 75–78, 105, 107, 112, 115, 120–21, 127–28, 130–31
        in the environment, 84
        in fathers and sons, 104–5
        in history, 7, 11
        in literature, 1, 4
        in men and women, 102–3
        in mothers and daughters, 106–8
        in obedience vs. disobedience to authority, 100, 102
        in prophecy, 15, 38, 95 n. 73, 104–5, 109, 114–15, 119–31
        in riddles, 18–19, 24–25, 27, 104–5, 126–28, 130
        role of hope in, 72–73, 75–76
        in the self and other, 112, 115
        in siblings, 108, 111
        in Stoic thought, 55, 57, 68
        in ten areas of life, 81
        in war and peace, 117–18
Medford, Massachusetts, 10
Meier, R., 44 n. 72
Meirope, Queen, 104
men and women, meaning vs. purpose in
    Adam-Eve, 102–3
    biblical narrative, 102–3
    Greek narrative, 102–3
    Prometheus-Pandora, 102–3
Menelaus, King, 33, 79, 116
Menoeceus, 29
Merope, 120
Metamorphoses (Ovid), 90 n. 44, 112
Metis, 15
Meursault, 1
Michigan, 60, 62, 64, 68
Middle Ages, 97
Middlesex, Massachusetts, 8, 10
Midrash, 85, 94, 100
Midrash Rabbah, 37, 44 n. 72
Milgram, Stanley, 99
Misra, Anuruddh K., 5, 7
Moab and Moabites [biblical], 107
moira (fate), 55, 79, 112, 121, 123, 126, 131
Moriah [biblical], 106
Moses, 3, 38–41, 96, 124
mothers and daughters, meaning vs. purpose in
    biblical narrative, 106–8
    Clytemnestra-Electra, 106–8

Greek narrative, 106–8
Naomi-Ruth, 106–8
Muntner, Seussman, 97
murder. *See* death
Mycenae, 90 n. 46
The Myth of Sisyphus (Camus), 1, 121

Naomi, 106–8
Narcissus
   approach of to life and death, 40
   meaning vs. purpose
      in Greek vs. biblical
         prophecies, 124
      in the self and other, 112, 114–15
   suicide of, 48, 56
   vs. Jonah, 40, 114–15, 124
Nathan, 119, 126, 129–30
Nathan, J., 5
Nazism, 2–3, 65, 99
Necessity, 4, 16, 54–55
Nehemiah, R., 110
Nemesis [god], 112, 114
Neptune, 88
Nero, 55
New Brick Church, 7, 11
New England, 7
New Mexico, 70
New Testament, 2, 7, 43, 101 n. 88
New York, 45 n. 72, 78
New York, New York, 78
Nietzsche, Friedrich, 131
Nineveh [biblical], 39–40, 113–15, 119
Niobic, 46
Noah, 74, 101, 110, 121
Noahide laws, 34
North Church, 8–9
Numbers, Book of, 38
Nuremberg, Germany, 99

Oakland County, Michigan, 62, 64
Obed, 108
obedience vs. disobedience to an authority, meaning vs. purpose in
   biblical narrative, 99–101
   God-Noah, 100–101
   Greek narrative, 99–101
   Zeus-Prometheus, 100–101
Odysseus, 31, 79, 87–89, 124 n. 17
Odyssey (Homer), 87–89, 91
Oedipus
   comparison to Patient Harry, 69
   hopelessness of, 74
   meaning vs. purpose
      in fathers and sons, 104–5
      in Greek vs. biblical
         prophecies, 126–28, 130
      in siblings, 108–11
      parables vs. riddles, 25–27, 104–5, 126–28, 130
   son of, 33 n. 20, 109–10
   suicide of, 29–30, 127
Oedipus in Jerusalem (Kaplan), 126, 130
Oedipus Redeemed (Kaplan), 130
Oedipus the King/Oedipus Rex (Sophocles), 29–30, 57, 74, 123
Oedipus the Teacher (Kaplan), 130
Old Testament. *See* Bible
Olympus, Mount, 73, 100, 102
Omri, General, 36
Oracle of Delphi, 82, 104, 126–27
Orestes, 107
Orion, 83
Orpah, 107
other and the self, meaning vs. purpose in
   biblical narrative, 113–15
   Greek narrative, 112–15
   Jonah, 113–15
   Narcissus, 112, 114–15
Ouranos, 15
Ovid, 48, 56, 90 n. 44, 112–13
Oxford Classical Dictionary, 87

Pan, 6
Pandora, 73–74, 102
parables vs. riddles, 18–27, 87, 89, 104–5, 124, 126–31
Paris [character], 116
Parmenides, 4
Passover, 93, 95–96
Paul Revere's Ride (Longfellow), 7–11
Paulina, 29, 55

peace and war, meaning vs. purpose in
 biblical narrative, 115–18
 David vs. Goliath, 116–17
 Greek narrative, 115–18
 Hector vs. Achilles, 116
Pelops, 88
Penobscot Expedition, 11 n. 25
Pentateuch. *See* Bible
Pentheus, King, 89, 90 n. 44
Persephone, 32, 75, 88
Persia, 6
Pesach. *See* Passover
Petronius, 91
Phaedra, 29, 31–32
Pheidippides (Browning), 6
Pheidippides, meaning vs. purpose of the run of, 4–7, 11, 72
Philistines, the, 36–38, 117
Philomela, 90 n. 45, 90 n. 47
The Phoenissae (Euripides), 29, 31
Pisa, 83
Plato, 83, 124–25
Plutarch, 28, 84
Poland, 2
Polybus, King, 104
Polyneices, 30, 109
Polyphemus, 89
Polyxena, 29, 32–34, 75–76
prayer of Maimonides, 97–99
Preuss, Jacob (Julius), 97
prevention, suicide
 as biblical approach, 4, 38–45, 48, 50, 62, 65–67, 71–72, 77–80
 case studies of, 60, 66 n. 5
 David, King, 38, 42
 Elijah, 38–39, 43, 78–80
 Harry, 68–71
 Job, 38, 41–42, 48–50, 62, 65–67, 71–72, 77
 Jonah, 38–40, 113–15
 lack of in Greek tragedies, 34, 55
 Moses, 38–41
 in movies, 78
 Rebecca, 38, 40
Priam, King, 32, 119
Procne, 90
Prometheus, 73, 100–102, 123

prophecy, meaning vs. purpose in
 Greek vs. biblical, 15, 38, 95 n. 73, 104–5, 109, 114–15, 119–31
Psalms, Book of, 38, 42, 96
Ptolemy, 43
purpose
 God as creator of man and his, 4, 13–14, 16–17, 25–27, 37, 47–51, 56–57, 77–78, 81–82, 84–86, 92–96, 98–101, 103, 105–7, 110–11, 113–18, 120–21, 124, 126, 129–31
 lack of leading to suicide, 2, 4, 12, 28, 30, 37, 43, 47–48, 50, 53, 56, 62, 67, 71–72, 77–80, 112, 114–15, 120–21, 127
 living with
  as biblical approach, 3–4, 7, 11, 13–14, 17–19, 25–28, 37, 43, 47–51, 56–57, 59, 66, 72–73, 75, 77–79, 81–82, 84–85, 87, 92–93, 95, 97, 99–100, 102–4, 106, 108, 110–11, 113–21, 124–27, 129–31
  in eating, 87–93, 95, 97
  in the environment, 82, 84–85
  in fathers and sons, 104, 106
  in Greek vs. biblical prophecies, 15, 38, 95 n. 73, 104–5, 109, 114–15, 119–31
  in history, 2–3, 7, 11
  in illness, 98–99
  Job as example of, 48–51, 62, 67, 71–73, 77, 131
  in literature, 3–4
  in men and women, 102–3
  in mothers and daughters, 106–8
  in obedience vs. disobedience to authority, 99–100, 102
  in the self and other, 112–15
  in siblings, 108, 110–11
  in Stoic vs. biblical thought, 52–58
  in war and peace, 116–18

meaning as consequence of, 4, 131
parable as, 18–19, 24–25, 27, 126, 129–30
of Paul Revere's ride, 7–12
of Pheidippides' run, 4–7, 11, 72
The Purpose Driven Life (Warren), 2
Pyrrha, 100–101
Pythagoras, 29
Pythia. *See* Oracle of Delphi

Ragesh (Razis), 43
Rashi, 26
Rebecca, 38, 40, 110–11
repentance/return. *See* teshuvah (repentance/return)
Revelation, Book of, 2
Revere, meaning vs. purpose of the ride of Paul, 7–12
Revere and Son, 11
Rhea, 109
riddles vs. parables, 18–27, 87, 89, 104–5, 124, 126–31
ride of Paul Revere, meaning vs. purpose of the, 7–12
Roman Empire, 84
Rome and Romans
    approach of to life and death, 28–29, 44, 53, 55, 57, 76–77, 127
    meaning vs. purpose
        in eating, 87, 90 n. 47, 91–92
        in the environment, 82–84
        in fathers and sons, 105
        in Greek vs. biblical prophecies, 127
        in illness, 97
    Stoicism, 53, 55, 57, 72
Rumpelstiltskin, 19–21, 24
run of Pheidippides, meaning vs. purpose of the, 4–7, 11, 72
Ruth, 106–8

Sabbath, the, 35, 44 n. 72, 93
Samaria [biblical], 95 n. 73
Samson, 35–37
Samuel 1, Book of, 14, 35, 57
Samuel 2, Book of, 35
Sanhedrin, 39, 126
Saragiotto, Bruno T., 5
Sarah, 26, 105, 110
Sarai. *See* Sarah
Satyricon, v. Dinner with Trimalchio (Petronius), 91
Saul, King, 35–38
Schwartz, Matthew B., 4, 93 n. 63, 97, 122, 131
Scintilla, 92
Scriptures, Hebrew (Torah). *See* Bible
Seder, 93, 95–96
Sefer Hachinuch, 85
self and other, meaning vs. purpose in the
    biblical narrative, 113–15
    Greek narrative, 112–15
    Jonah, 113–15
    Narcissus, 112, 114–15
self-sacrifice. *See* altruistic suicide
Semachot [Talmudic tractate], 44 n. 72
Seneca, 29, 55, 72
Seneca the Elder, 54
The Seven Against Thebes (Aeschylus), 33 n. 20
Shabbat [Talmudic tractate], 86
Shakespeare, William, 90 n. 47
Shapiro, Michael, xii
Shema, 76
Shemesh, Yael, 43
Shestov, Lev, 4
Shoham, Shlomo G., 89
siblings, meaning vs. purpose in
    biblical narrative, 108, 110–11
    Greek narrative, 108–11
Sinai, Mount, 3
Sisyphus, 1, 120–21, 123, 128
Sky, 15–16, 109
Slater, Phillip, 6–7, 13
Snell, Bruno, 14
Socrates, 29, 54, 124–25
Solomon, King, 57, 130
Soloveitchik, R. Joseph B., 86
sons and fathers, meaning vs. purpose in
    Abraham-Isaac, 104–6
    biblical narrative, 104–6
    Greek narrative, 104–5
    Laius-Oedipus, 104–5

Sophocles
    hope as illusion in tragedies of, 74
    riddles in tragedies of, 18, 126–27
    search for meaning in tragedies of, 29–31, 33, 34 n. 21, 37, 57, 72, 75
    suicides in tragedies of, 28–31, 33, 34 n. 21, 37, 38 n. 38
    value in misery in tragedies of, 123
Spain, 45 n. 72
Spanish Inquisition, 45 n. 72
Sparta, Greece, 5, 116
Sphinx, 25–27, 104, 128
Stoicism
    in clinical cases, 59, 68
    meaning vs. purpose in, 48, 52–58, 78–79
    view of death in, 48, 52–56, 68, 72, 77–78
    Zeno as founder of, 46, 72
Strabo, 83
The Stranger (Camus), 1
suicide. *see also* death
    Abimelech, 35–36
    Ahitophel, 35–36
    Ajax, 29, 31, 33–34, 37, 79–80, 124 n. 17
    Alcestis, 29, 32
    altruistic, 29, 33, 35, 37, 43, 76
    anomic, 29–30
    Antigone, 29–30
    assisted, 36, 59–62, 64–68
    in the Bible, 34–38, 43–44
    Charlotte, 59–68, 72, 77
    clinical cases, 59–72, 77, 98 n. 81
    covenantal, 37
    Deianeira, 29–31
    egoistic, 29–31, 33, 35–37
    Eurydice, 29–30
    Evadne, 29
    in Greek tragedy, 1, 28–35, 37, 38 n. 38, 44, 46–48, 50, 52–56, 61–62, 67–69, 72, 76, 79–80, 109, 112, 114–15, 120–23, 124 n. 17, 127
    Haemon, 29–30
    Heracles, 29–32
    Hermione, 29

Iphigenia, 29, 33–34
Jocasta, 25, 29–30, 109
Judas Iscariot, 43
lack of purpose leading to, 2, 4, 12, 28, 30, 37, 43, 47–48, 50, 53, 56, 62, 67, 71–72, 77–80, 112, 114–15, 120–21, 127
Macaria, 29, 32–34
meaninglessness leading to, 1–2, 4, 12, 28–37, 41–43, 47–48, 50, 55–56, 61–62, 65–68, 71–72, 76–78, 112, 115, 120–21, 127
Menoeceus, 29
Oedipus, 29–30, 127
Phaedra, 29, 31–32
Polyxena, 29, 32–34, 76
prevention. *see* prevention, suicide
Samson, 35–37
Saul, 35–38
Saul's armor bearer, 35–37
Zimri, 35–36
The Sunset Limited, 78–80
The Suppliants (Euripides), 29, 31
syllogisms, biblical vs. Greek, 124–26
syndrome, Zeno, 59
Syrians, the, 43

T4, 65
Tabor, James, 56, 62
Talmud, 34, 44, 74, 85–86, 97
Tamora, Queen, 90 n. 47
Tanakh. *See* Bible
Tantalus, 88–89
Tarfon, R., 123
Tarshish [biblical], 39, 113–14
Tartarus, 15, 109
Tate, Sharon, 2
Teiresias, 120, 127–28
Telepylos, 89
Temple, Holy, 35, 43, 113
Terah, 105
Tereus, 90
teshuvah (repentance/return), 40, 42, 113–14, 119, 126, 129–30
Teucer, 79
Thebes and Thebans, 104–5, 109, 126–28, 130
Theodectes, 26

Theogony (Hesiod), 14–15
Theseus, King, 31, 90 n. 46
Thessaly [historical], 32
Thucydides
Thyestes, 90
Tiresias, 112
Titans, 15, 109
Titus, 90 n. 47
Titus Andronicus (Shakespeare), 90 n. 47
tohu vovohu (unformed), 16–17, 25–26, 82, 84
Toller, Ernst, 45 n. 72
Torah (Hebrew Scriptures). *See* Bible
The Trachinae (Sophocles), 29–30, 75
Trimalchio, 91–92, 95
Trojan War, 79
Troy and the Trojans, 32–33, 75–76, 88, 116, 119, 124 n. 17
Truth, 19
Tusculan Disputations (Cicero), 54
Tzetzes, Johannes, 124

Uranus, 109
Uriah the Hittite, 129

Venus, 101
Verdun, France, 45 n. 72

war and peace, meaning vs. purpose in
    biblical narrative, 115–18
        David vs. Goliath, 116–17
    Greek narrative, 115–18
        Hector vs. Achilles, 116
Warren, Kay, 3
Warren, Rick, 2–3
Wars of the Jews (Josephus), 43
Warsaw Ghetto, 45 n. 72
Wayne State University, 60, 63
Weininger, Otto, 45 n. 72
The White Album (the Beatles), 2

Wolterstorff, Nicholas, 4, 131
women and men, meaning vs. purpose in
    Adam-Eve, 102–3
    biblical narrative, 102–3
    Greek narrative, 102–3
    Prometheus-Pandora, 102–3
world to come, 44 n. 72
World War II, 2, 45 n. 72

Xerxes, King, 83

Yahweh. *See* God
Yale University, 4
Yemima, 50
Yerushalmi, Yosef H., 126
York, England, 45 n. 72

Zeno the Stoic of Citium
    syndrome, 59
    view of death of, 29, 46–53, 55–56, 61–62, 67–68, 72, 75–77
    vs. Job, 41–42, 46–52, 72, 77, 131
Zeus
    and death of Zeno, 47, 56
    Greek view of creation, 15–16
    Greek view of hope, 73
    meaning vs. purpose
        in eating, 88, 90 n. 46, 94
        in the environment, 82–83, 86
        in fathers and sons, 104
        in Greek vs. biblical prophecies, 130
        in men and women, 102
        in obedience vs. disobedience to authority, 100–101
        in siblings, 109, 120
Zimri, 35–36
Zophar, 49
Zygelbojm, Samuel, 45 n. 72

www.ingramcontent.com/pod-product-compliance
Lightning Source LLC
Chambersburg PA
CBHW051938160426
43198CB00013B/2211